ASSIGNMENTS IN MUSICAL THEATRE
Acting and Directing

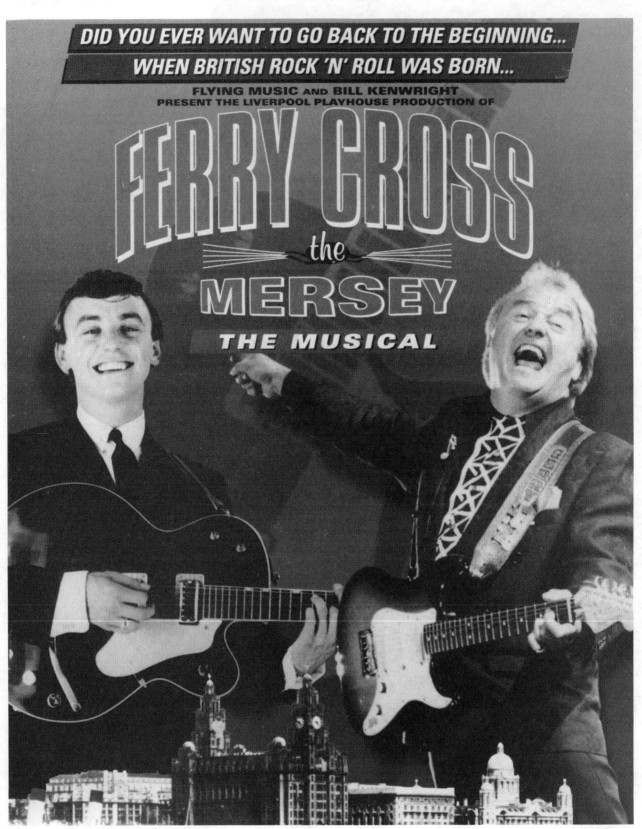

Plate 1. FERRY CROSS THE MERSEY *is a musical that bridges several styles creating its own musical style. It is a biographical story, a concert, a revue and all blend to create this potentially exciting format. Gerry Marsden, right, plays himself, the narrator, and Carl Kirshner, left, plays young Gerry. Courtesy of Derek Nicol, Paul Walden, Flying Music Company Co, Ltd. and the designers of the flyer, Dewynters PLC.*

ASSIGNMENTS IN MUSICAL THEATRE
Acting and Directing

by
Jacque Wheeler
and
Haller Laughlin

PLAYERS PRESS

Australia   **Canada**   **United Kingdom**   **United States**

ASSIGNMENTS IN MUSICAL THEATRE

ISBN 0-88734-676-6
Library of Congress Catalogue Number: 97-4037

PLAYERS PRESS, Inc.
P. O. Box 1132
Studio City CA 91614-0132 U.S.A.

Design & Edit: William-Alan Landes
Paste-Up: Chris Cordero
Typset: Sharon Landes

Acknowledgments

The Authors would like to thank the following for all their help in the completion of this text: Deborah Morgan, Karen Stigura, David Blakeman, all the students in Stage Movement at Valdosta State University, DeRon Coppage, Sharon, and, especially, William.

Simultaneously Published
U.S.A., U.K., Canada and Australia
Printed in the U.S.A.

Library of Congress Cataloging-in-Publication Data

Wheeler, Jacque
    Assignments in musical theatre : acting and directing / by Jacque Wheeler and Haller Laughlin
       p.   cm.
    Includes bibliographical references and index.
    ISBN 0-88734-676-6 (alk. paper)
    1. Acting in musical theatre.   2. Musical theatre--Production and direction.   I. Laughlin, Haller. II. Title.
MT956.W45 1997   97-4037
792' .028--dc21   CIP
                                                        MN

Dedicated to:

C. Wiandt from Haller
Randy, Melissa, Kit and Megan from Jacque

CONTENTS

Illustrations   viii

Introduction   ix

Sources   xii

1   A Method For Musical Theatre Madness   1

2   Learning the Language   5

3   Musical Movement: Establishment of Character Through Movement   21

4   Acting the Song   43

5   Acting the Dance   57

6   Making Musical Comedy Comic   71

7   Meeting the Demands of Musical Drama   99

8   The Magic Kingdom: Operetta   111

9   The Latest Arrival: Broadway Opera   119

10   Highlighting the Hybrids: The Revue, the Symphonic Drama and the Play with Music   129

11   Putting It All Together: The Audition   141

Glossary   151

Appendix I - Audition Material   147

      Young Juvenile (6-13)   151

      Juvenile (14-20)   151

      Romantic Lead Female   152

      Romantic Lead Male   153

      Character Female (20-40)   154

      Character Male (20-40)   155

      Character Female (40+)   155

      Character Male (40+)   156

      Comic Songs   157

      Songs for Dances   158

Appendix II - Libretto Sources   159

Appendix III - Children's Theatre Musical Scores   169

Bibliography   173

Index   175

ILLUSTRATIONS

FIGURE		PAGE
P-1	*Ferry Cross The Mersey*	ii
P-2	*State Fair*, Long Beach Convention & Entertainment Center	xi
1	*You're A Good Man Charlie Brown*, Players U.S.A.	xiv
2	Leonard Bernstein rehearsing *West Side Story*	2
3	Agnes De Mille working with Dancers	3
4	Jerry Orbach and Gwen Verdon, *Chicago*	4
5	Harold Prince and Joel Grey, *Silverlake*	6
6	Washington Senators from *Damn Yankees*	8
7	*Yankee Doodle Dandy*	18
8	Ray Bolger in *On Your Toes*	20
9	Characters Stand in *Rumpelstiltskin*	22
10	Actor demonstrates neutral energy	24
11	Body alignment chart	25
12	Jekyll Island Musical Theatre Festival, *Oklahoma!*	26
13	Releasing Shoulder Tension	29
14	Yawn Stretch	29
15	Illustrative Gesture	31
16	Indicative Gesture	31
17	Forceful Gesture, *Jacque Brel is Alive and Well and Living in Paris,* Players U.S.A.	32
18	Two photos of the Cat from the Players U.S.A. *Peter n'the Wolf*	35
19	Bob Hope, Jimmy Durante and Ethel Merman, *Red Hot and Blue*	43
20	Giant and Beanseller from the Players U.S.A. *Jack n'the Beanstalk*	44
21	Julie Andrews in Rehearsal	46
22	George M. Cohan from *Little Johnny Jones*	50
23	George M. Cohan, *I'd Rather Be Right*	50
24	Dance at Full Energy	56
25	Dance Mood	56
26	Three photos: Minimal Energy, Moderate Energy, and Maximum Energy	58
27	Bob Fosse and Gwen Verdon, Rehearsal	60
28	*Chorus Line*, New York Shakespeare Festival	61
29	Billy Daniels and Pearl Bailey, *Hello, Dolly!*	62
30	Working in a rehearsal skirt	66
31	Lions,	68
32	Sailors,	68
33	Tramps and Sailors	68
34	*Kiss Me Kate*, the Megan Theatre	70
P-3	*Cabaret*, Long Beach Civic Light Opera	72
P-4	*Annie*, Long Beach Convention & Entertainment Center	73
P-5	*Leave It To Jane*	80
35	Poster for *Oh, Boy*	89
36	Two photos from *Tall Betsy and the Crackerbarrel Tales*	97
37	*Cabaret*, Valdosta State University	98
38	*Carousel*, open body position	100
39	"Isn't It Great (to Be Married)," *Very Good, Eddie*	102
40	Robert Hays and Karen Flathers, *Brigadoon*	103
41	*Gypsy*, Glassboro Summer Theatre	107
42	*The Student Prince*, Los Angeles Music Center	110
43	*H.M.S. Pinafore*, North Carolina School of the Arts	112
44	*Pirates of Penzance*, Valdosta State University	115
45	A design for Cat makeup, *Stage Make-up Techniques*	118
46	*Joseph and the Amazing Technicolor Dream Coat*, Jekyll Island Musical Theatre Festival	121
47	*Nunsense*, Jekyll Island Musical Theatre Festival	122
48	Christina Avila and Grant Goodeve, *Jacques Brel is Alive and Well and Living in Paris*	128
49	*She Stoops to Conquer*, Valdosta State University	131
50	*Nunsense*, Jekyll Island Musical Theatre Festival	133
51	An audition, *Once Upon a Mattress*	142
52	*Sunday in the Park with George*, Showtime	144
53	*Show Boat*, Long Beach C.L.O.	158
54	*Cinderella*, Long Beach Convention & Entertainment Center	174

INTRODUCTION

Since the mid 1960s the growth of musical theatre production by high schools, colleges, universities, community, summer, and resident theatres has been phenomenal. During this time of prolific production, unfortunately, the requisites of musical theatre performance have not been carefully analyzed. In general, it has been the assumption that the acting in musical theatre is less demanding than acting in non-musical theatre and merely a combination of energy and personality. On the contrary, musical theatre acting should be perceived as more demanding than non-musical theatre acting.

Not only does the musical actor need all the requisite skills of the non-musical actor, but he needs additional technical skills in vocal and bodily control and flexibility. The musical theatre actor also needs the imaginative ability to analyze material that is exceedingly complex in structure, tone, and environment. There is little material to help musical theatre actors and directors approach musical theatre scripts and performances from this multi-level perspective.

Most published work has either a largely professional perspective or emphasizes either the singing or acting perspectives, without integrating both. None offers a structured approach to musical theatre acting that is specifically directed toward use in an educational setting or in the type of workshop structure employed for the development of young professionals. We perceive the necessity of offering a text which presents a specific structure for students/ teachers/ directors that gives a basis and starting place from which to explore musical theatre acting in both classroom and workshop settings.

Although this book appears to emphasize only acting assignments, these same assignments are valuable to the director as well. Certainly in many cases the director serves as an acting coach, particularly in high school, college and community productions. Directors as well as actors need a clear understanding of the structure of musical theatre librettos and of show layouts as described in the text. The answers to questions of character motivation and development are ones on which director and actor must agree.

Therefore, *Assignments In Musical Theatre* emphasizes pre-performance analysis for both aspiring musical theatre actors and directors. The book is the outcome of our many years of experience as musical theatre performers, directors, teachers of musical theatre, and coordinators of musical theatre workshops and curriculums. We have learned a great deal and hope to contribute to the exploration of musical theatre performance in a way that saves you both time and unnecessary effort. We feel that the material in this text will prove invaluable in assisting the establishment of a strong musical performance technique, without which no performer, however talented, can be successful.

A musical performing class must have an assigned pianist/accompanist both during class time and for student preparation of scenes. This accompanist need not attend every class, but should be available for a minimum of 50% of the class sessions. Students need to learn to work economically with an accompanist, making the most of the least amount of time. Some work with practice tapes is expected but not to the exclusion of work with the accompanist. In addition, it is suggested that a vocal coach be invited to attend class and give comments when appropriate.

It is imperative that the student have access to a well sized collection of musical librettos and scores. The following is a suggested list, based principally on script and score accessibility.

Ain't Misbehavin'	The King and I	Phantom of the Opera
Ain't Supposed to Die a Natural Death	Kismet	Plain and Fancy
	Kiss Me Kate	Pretzels
Allegro	The Last Sweet Days of Isaac	Promenade
Aspects of Love	Leave It to Jane	Promises, Promises
Baker Street	Li'l Abner	Purlie
Carousel	Little Johnny Jones	Raisin
Celebration	Little Mary Sunshine	Roar of the Greasepaint
Chicago	Little Women	Rose Marie
The Chocolate Soldier	Lock Up Your Daughters	Robert and Elizabeth
Curley McDimple	Lovely Ladies, Kind Gentlemen	The Rothschilds
Dames at Sea	Mack and Mabel	Runaway
Diamond Studs	The Mad Show	Seesaw
Do Patent Leather Shoes Really Reflect Up	Maggie Flynn	Seventeen
	Mame	70, Girls, 70
Donnybrook	Man of LaMancha	Shenandoah
Don't Bother Me I Can't Cope	The Man with a Load of Mischief	Sherlock Holmes in The Deerstalker
Drat! The Cat	Me and Juliet	
Fashion	The Me Nobody Knows	Shogun
The Fire Fly	Meet Me in St. Louis	Showboat
First Impressions	The Merry Widow	Singing in the Rain
Golden Boy	Minnie's Boys	Skyscraper
Golden Rainbow	Miss Saigon	Something's Afoot
Goldilocks	My Fair Lady	South Pacific
Good News	Naughty Marietta	Stop the World, I Want to Get Off
Goodtime Charley	New Girl in Town	The Streets of New York
Grand Hotel	Nunsense	Sunday in the Park with George
The Grand Tour	Of Thee I Sing	Sweeney Todd
The Grass Harp	Oh Boy!	Sweet Charity
Grease	Oklahoma!	They're Playing Our Song
Gypsy	Oliver	Three Wishes for Jamie
Hello, Dolly!	On the Twentieth Century	Via Galactica
Henry, Sweet Henry	Over Here	Walking Happy
How Now, Dow Jones	Paint Your Wagon	The Wiz
Into the Woods	Pajama Game	You're A Good Man, Charlie Brown
I Love My Wife	Pal Joey	
Jacques Brel Is Alive And Well...	Peter Pan	Zorba

The following are additional sources for the texts of certain musicals:

Bordman, Gerald. *American Musical Theatre. A Chronical.* New York: Oxford University Press, 1978.

Laughlin, Haller, and Wheeler, Randy. *Producing the Musical.* Connecticut: Greenwood Press, 1984.

Richards, Stanley, Ed. *The Great Musicals of the American Theatre.* Vol. 2. Radnor, Pennsylvania: Chilton Book Company, 1976.
_____. *Great Rock Musicals.* New York: Stein and Day, 1979.

_____. *Ten Great Musicals of the American Theatre.* Radnor, Pennsylvania: Chilton Book Company, 1973.

Rodgers, Richard, and Hammerstein, II, Oscar. *Six Plays by Rodgers and Hammerstein.* New York: Random House, 1963.

Plate 2. State Fair, *Long Beach Civic Light Opera's West Coast Premiere of the Rodgers and Hammerstein musical. Photo by Spike Nannarello.*

The following sources for obtaining scripts, scores, and recordings are the most dependable. Instructors should expect a delay of four to six weeks for delivery of most materials within a country and 10-12 weeks if coming from another country.

U.S.A.
Colony Records & Music
1619 Broadway
New York NY 10036
(212) 265-2050

Players Press, Inc.
P.O. Box 1132
Studio City, CA 91614-0132
(818) 789-4980

Music Exchange
151 West 46th Street
10th Floor
New York NY 10036
(212) 354-5858

Drama Book Shop
134 Ninth Street
San Francisco, CA 94103
(415) 255-0604

SOUTH AFRICA
Fogarty's Bookshop
Main Street at Market Sq.
P. O. Box 1881
Port Elizabeth

CANADA
Mayfair Cornerstone
17600 Yonge Street
Newmarket, ON L3Y 2T2

Stratford Festival Bookshop
55 Queen Street
P. O. Box 520
Stratford ON N5A 6V2

AUSTRALIA
UNIBOOKS
P. O. Box 498
Union Bldg., Univ. of Adelaide
Adelaide S.A. 5001
(08) 223 4366

Fine Music
20-22 McKillop St.
Melbourne, 3000

Performing Arts Bookshop
7th Floor, 280 Pitt St.
Sydney, N.S.W. 2000

U.K./EUROPE
Players Press, Ltd.
20 Park Drive
Romford
Essex RM1 4LH, U. K.

International Theatre &
Film Bookshop
Leidseplein 26
1017 PT
Amsterdam NEDERLANDS

Theaterjornet
Vesterbrogode 175
DK-1800, Frderiksberg
Copenhagen
DENMARK

JAPAN
Asano Bookshop
6-12 Hoyato-Cho
Showa-Ku, Nagoya

NEW ZEALAND
Bennets
P. O. Box 138
Private Bay 11-004
Palmerston North
(06) 358-3009

ASSIGNMENTS IN MUSICAL THEATRE
Acting and Directing

Figure 1. Patty, Lucy and Charlie Brown in YOU'RE A GOOD MAN, CHARLIE BROWN, *produced by Players U.S.A.*

Chapter One

A "METHOD" FOR MUSICAL THEATRE MADNESS

Voice. Body. Imagination. These are the tools of the actor in the creation of every role. In creating characters for musical theatre, a great deal more emphasis has traditionally been placed on the voice and body. The singer has to stay on pitch, the tempos must be consistent, the singer and the orchestra must be together, the song must be heard, and the lyrics understood. The dancer must have turn-out, extension, tap skills, jazz skills, and a good ballet line. The music in the musical theatre repertoire ranges from popular to jazz to classical, and the actor needs to feel comfortable in all these genres. The singer and the dancer then need flexibility and dexterity in both voice and body. As a singer, the actor needs a singing technique - a technique to help sustain those notes held for eight counts after a long musical phrase. He needs a dance technique to do a pirouette, an arabesque, or a time step. So the musical theatre actor takes voice lessons and dance classes. Often, however, in the quest for a high C or the ability to kick the leg over the head, the actor's third tool, the imagination, gets short shrift. Frequently musical theatre acting is thought of as singing, dancing, and speaking with energy. The actor's imagination has received little attention, and he wanders through the rehearsal period uncomfortable but not really knowing why.

It is in the actor's mind, in the imagination, that the singing, dancing, and speaking become a coordinated whole. It is in the imagination that the element of character *motivation* is added. It is this motivation for the character as determined by the actor (in coordination with the director) that governs all the choices made about the character. It is not only important **how** the actor sings the song but **why** he is singing the song. What is he trying to accomplish by singing the song? It is not only important **how** he dances the number but **why** he dances in the first place. Certainly musicals are not realistic dramas, but there is a logic within the reality of each musical theatre text which the actor needs to perceive, even though that logic may be illogical in realistic terms.

Our purpose here is to offer explanations, suggestions, definitions, and exercises which will lead the actor in the development of a musical theatre acting technique. Through the exercises in this text, an actor will learn a variety of approaches to a musical theatre script, which are determined by the show type. He will learn how to analyze both the songs and the character in the text. A series of worksheets is provided to guide the actor in completing the assignments.

The labyrinth of musical theatre literature can be confusing. The terminology is not universally clear. What is a musical? What is musical comedy? What is musical drama? In essence, musical theatre performance requires not **one** style but **many** styles, depending on the show type. The performance skills required in musical theatre acting are as broad as those required in any period styles acting class. The actor must additionally be facile with more realistic approaches as well. Even techniques proposed by Stanislavsky have a place in musical theatre acting. The basic question for the actor whether in a nonmusical or a musical situation remains "What would I do **if** I were this character in this situation?" The use of an actor's memory of his past experiences and emotions is as appropriate for the actor in musical theatre as for the actor in nonmusical theatre. The sense of **ensemble**, of a group of people working together for a common goal, listening and responding to each other, is as important in musical theatre as in nonmusical theatre. The character's inner thoughts, his **subtext**, serve as motivation for lines in musical as well as nonmusical texts.

It is the intention of this text to encourage the actor to make specific choices through the performance of the exercises which follow. It is the making of specific choices which leads to the creation of clear, interesting and multi-dimensional characters, not only in musical theatre, but also in nonmusical theatre. It is through the choices the actor makes that the audience perceives the motivation of the character and the actor determines the motivation of the character. A clear perception of what motivates the character increases not only audience understanding and empathy for the character but the actor's understanding of the character as well.

The exercises combine nonmusical techniques with the essential integration of singing the songs and dancing the dances - skills not consistently required in the nonmusical. They also serve to encourage the actor to develop the heightened energy and physical stamina required in musical theatre performance.

We do not suppose that any class or workshop could com-

FIGURE 2. Composer Leonard Bernstein working with the chorus of WEST SIDE STORY.

plete all 26 assignments within the course of a single term. Rather the instructor and the actor can choose the assignments which seem most pertinent to the skills of the actors in the group, even repeating some if necessary.

With the aid of *Assignments in Musical Theatre*, the actor will have a much greater facility in approaching any role in the musical theatre repertoire.

FIGURE 3. *Agnes De Mille working dancers for* 110 IN THE SHADE.

Figure 4.   CHICAGO. Directed and choreographed by Bob Fosse. Jerry Orbach and Gwen Verdon

Chapter Two

LEARNING THE LANGUAGE

The musical theatre actor must begin the study of his craft by becoming familiar with acting styles pertinent to various types of musical theatre — musical comedy, musical drama, operetta, Broadway opera, revue, symphonic drama, and the hybrid known as the "play with music." The student must also be familiar with interpretive as well as physical and vocal techniques which are a part of the musical theatre performers' equipment, and with the methods of developing these towards successful performances.

In developing any technique, the actor must be able to analyze for himself the elements which combine to create the character. In musical theatre performance the first such element is **the show type**. There are seven types of musical librettos. They include:

1. Musical Comedy
2. Musical Drama
3. Operetta
4. Broadway Opera
5. Symphonic Drama
6. Play with Music
7. Revue

A **Musical Comedy** has a loosely constructed plot, interspersed with extended bits of comedy business and vehicle numbers for specific, and often, non-related performing styles. There is little integration between music and libretto. Examples are *Anything Goes, Panama Hattie, No, No, Nanette, Of Thee I Sing,* and *Wonderful Town.*

In **Musical Drama**, score and plot support each other. Music and libretto are well integrated. There is little or no extraneous material, and there are complex character development and integrated subplots. Dialogue may be minimized. Examples are *Carousel, West Side Story, La Cage aux Folles, Gypsy,* and *Barnum.*

The **Operetta** is romantic and lyrical, has more music than dialogue, and features melodramatic stereotypes. Music is of primary importance. The score is complex, making frequent use of trios, quartets, sextets, and intricate choral numbers. The setting is often foreign. Examples are *The Merry Widow, Kismet, Pirates of Penzance, A Little Night Music,* and *The Mystery of Edwin Drood.*

The **Broadway Opera** also emphasizes difficult music, but it is music derived from popular sources and spectacular in content and treatment. There is little or no dialogue and dance is integrated or minimal. Examples are *Porgy and Bess, Evita, Joseph and the Amazing Technicolor Dreamcoat, Les Miserables,* and *Phantom of the Opera.*

The **Symphonic drama** is usually patriotic or historic in plot and combines all of the elements of theatre: song, dance, drama, and spectacle. The music reflects the time and location of the production, whether it is original or period music. Examples are *Lone Star, The Legend of Daniel Boone, Sword of Peace,* and *Unto These Hills.*

In the **Play With Music**, the plot is not dependent on the music and musical numbers are few, used primarily to illustrate or comment on the action. Examples are *Good Woman of Setzuan , Collette,* and *Johnny Johnson.*

A **Revue** is a combination of musical numbers, sketches, and routines based on a theme. The characters may or may not be continuing. The tone is sometimes satiric, sometimes retrospective. Examples are *You're a Good Man ,Charlie Brown, Ain't Misbehavin',* and *Jacques Brel Is Alive and Well and Living in Paris.*

FIGURE 5. Harold Prince (Left) and Joel Grey (Right) for the New York City Opera's production of Kurt Weill's SILVERLAKE.

At the conclusion of the exercises in this text, the actor will find a listing of musicals according to show type. A word of caution is important. The classifications indicate these authors' perception of the dominant elements of the libretto and score, causing the musical to be defined in a certain category. Few musicals, however, exemplify only one show type. Most musicals have a predominant emphasis with elements of other show types present as well.

Having mastered the categories of musical theatre, the second element a performer must analyze is the **show layout**. The show layout refers to the types of songs in the musical and the order in which they appear in the production. The types of songs found in musical theatre are:

1. Ballad
2. Charm
3. Rhythm
4. Comedy
    a. Short Joke
    b. Long Joke
    c. Patter
5. Eleven O'Clock Number
6. Musical scene

A **Ballad** is a song with a recurrent theme, musically slower and longer than the other show songs. It may be narrative, romantic, a soliloquy, or a character song. Examples are "Tonight" and "Hello, Young Lovers."

In a **Charm** song the music is delicate and light and the music and lyrics are equally important. Charm songs are optimistic, shorter than other show songs, and the songs which may achieve the most popularity outside the show. Examples are "Sixteen Going on Seventeen" and "More I Cannot Wish You."

A **Rhythm** song is primarily carried along or propelled by a dominant and regular musical beat. Examples are "Anything Goes" and "America."

There are three types of **Comedy** songs.

a. Short Joke: The choruses are brief, offering a repeated phrase at the end, thus allowing the audience time to laugh. An example is "Bewitched, Bothered and Bewildered."

b. Long Joke: A careful narrative builds to a surprise punch line. These are usually long songs, very difficult to do successfully. An example is "My Mother's Wedding Day."

c. Patter: A comic duet or solo in which the singers alternate verses or a quickly paced soliloquy in which the lyric is more important than the music. Examples are "Anything You Can Do I Can Do Better," and "Trouble."

An **Eleven O'Clock Number** is a showstopper scheduled late in the show to re-awaken the audience's enthusiasm. It is a star turn usually, though not always. Examples are "The Last Midnight," "Rose's Turn," "If He Walked Into My Life," and "So Long Dearie."

A "**Musical Scene**" is a sequence which combines music, pantomime, dialogue, dance, or stylized movement. Some examples are "Why Can't the English," the "Tonight" reprise, "I Put My Hand In," and "There's Gotta be Something Better Than This."

Once the actor perceives the overall show type and song layout of the libretto and score, he needs to focus on the musical numbers in which he is specifically involved., His songs should be analyzed in terms of the response desired from the singing of the song. What does the character hope to achieve by singing this song?

To aid in determining this goal, the musical theatre actor needs to be able to analyze the **song** and the **song layout**. A **song** is the musical setting of a lyric. A musical performer should think of a song as an elongated speech which creates instant atmosphere. A single song can do the work of an entire scene in a non-musical production. The **song layout** is composed of an introduction, vamp, verse, chorus, air, and rideout, all of which must be analyzed for tempo, mood, relationship to scene, integration in it, character who sings it, and style.

The **Introduction** is the beginning of a song and establishes rhythmic, melodic and harmonic material. A song **Vamp** is an instrumental, harmonic, and rhythmic section of a song which is repeated as needed. A **Vamp** is always indicated by repeat signs (double bar and dots). The **Vamp** may also set the key in which the song is sung, the tempo for the listener, and create the environment of the song. The length of the **Vamp** depends on the time the singer needs to prepare for the song. It may sometimes occur under the

Figure 6. The Washington Senators from Old Globe, San Diego, production of DAMN YANKEES: from left to right, Jeff Blumekrantz, Scott Wise, Gregory Ibara and Dick Latessa.

dialogue that precedes a song. The **verse** introduces and develops the subject of the song. It is melodically second to the **chorus**, which introduces and develops the main melodic theme of the song, and is the most repeated section of the song.

Air is the musical space without lyric that appears between the musical phrases of the song, between the verse and the chorus, after the vamp, before the rideout, and creates implicit character and emotional cues. **Rideout** is a reverse vamp. It ends each chorus and, finally, the song, and can range from one to many bars, although rarely longer than four. Inside the song it allows for applause or laughter, and following the song it should excite the audience to applause. A musical performer should be able to scan the songs within the musical and diagram each according to these.

In order to fully analyze the song and the song layout, the actor must be familiar with the following musical terms:

TIME SIGNATURE: a sign given at the beginning of a composition to indicate its meter.

MEASURE: the division of beat patterns indicated in music by bar lines; ordinarily recur consistently throughout a given composition.

FLATS AND SHARPS: used to indicate key signatures.
SHARP: raises the tone by a semitone and looks like [♯].

FLAT: lowers the tone by a semitone and looks like [♭].

NOTE: a symbol with a corresponding value and rest.
WHOLE, HALF, QUARTER, EIGHTH: four types of notes.

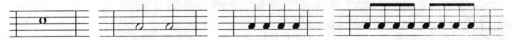

REST: a sign indicating that for a specified time, the music ceases but corresponds to a note value.

WHOLE, HALF, QUARTER, EIGHTH: four types of rests.

TRIPLET: a group of three notes to be performed in place of one or two of the same value, indicated by a numerical 3 and usually a slur.

DIAPHRAGM: the muscle used for support of the vocal sound.

RANGE: the form of classification used in identifying a voice type. Women's ranges include soprano, mezzo and alto. Men's ranges include tenor, baritone, and bass.

VOCALIZE: exercise used for practice in the production of vocal sound and for extension of range.

METER: in a given composition, the basic grouping of beats and accents found in each measure and as indicated by the time signature.

BEAT: the temporal unit of a composition as represented by the up and down movement of a conductor's hand.

DOTTED NOTE: a note having a dot at its right side, which adds to the note one half of its value.

PITCH: a term referring to the high-low quality of a musical sound.

OCTAVE: the interval embracing eight diatonic tones.

ACCOMPANIMENT: the musical background provided for a principal part, and may be performed by a piano or an orchestra.

Each staff is composed of 5 lines and 4 spaces. The names of lines and spaces for each clef are: **Bass clef**: G, B, D, F, A, and A, C, E, G. **Treble clef**: E, G, B, D, F, and F, A, C, E.

The last element but certainly not the least that the actor needs to be aware of is the libretto. The **libretto** is the script or the book for the musical. Many current librettos are based on novels, stories, plays, biographies, and films for which the action has been highly compressed, and often humor is added. A musical performer would be advised to investigate if the libretto is based on such a source and to note changes and additions that distinguish it from the original.

Assignment 1
Musical Oral Report

Choose a musical from the class reserve list. Make sure that you have access to score, libretto, and a recording. Read, listen, and analyze all three thoroughly. Present to the class an oral report which includes the following information:

1. Musical title and type.

2. A brief background of the author, composer, and lyricist.

3. A brief list of locations and times of action.

4. A list of the central characters, categorizing each in a brief phrase.

5. A brief outline of the plot by act.

6. The Show Layout by act.

7. Specific comments about the furthering of plot and character in dance sequences.

8. An evaluation of the musical (success of theme, artistic success, contributions of the musical to the contemporary musical scene; consult reviews of the original production and any subsequent revivals).

NOTES:

_____

_____

_____

_____

_____

_____

_____

_____

_____

_____

Assignment 2
Song Layout

Select a song from another class member's oral report and diagram it.

Introduction: Measure ____ to Measure ____
Vamp: Measure ____ to Measure ____
Verse: Measure ____ to Measure ____
               Measure ____ to Measure ____
               Measure ____ to Measure ____
               Measure ____ to Measure ____

Chorus: Measure ____ to Measure ____
               Measure ____ to Measure ____
               Measure ____ to Measure ____
               Measure ____ to Measure ____

Final Rideout*:   Measure ____ to Measure ___

Note: interior rideouts and air passages where they occur within the song.

Sample Assignment   Song Layout for "THE YANKEE DOODLE BOY"

Introduction: Measure__1__to Measure_14_
Vamp: Measure__0__to Measure__0__   (This song does not contain a vamp.)
Verse: Measure_15_to Measure_46_

Chorus: Measure__51_to Measure_82_

Final Rideout: Measure_83__ to Measure_84_

Interior Rideout: Measure_47__ to Measure_50_

Air Passages: Measure_46__; Measure_62_; Measure_66_; Measure_70_;
                   Measure_74__; Measure_82_; Measure_84_.

The music from *THE YANKEE DOODLE BOY* is reprinted here to serve as a sample in completing Assignment 2. The measures have been numbered for the student. The completed diagram for the Assignment 2 Sample appears on the previous page.

THE YANKEE DOODLE BOY

George M. Cohan

Born on the Fourth of Ju - ly. _____ I've
got a Yan - kee Doo - dle sweet - - heart,
She's my Yan - kee Doo - dle joy. _____ Yan - kee Doo - dle
came to Lon - don, Just to ride the pon - ies; I am the

Yan-kee Doo-dle Boy._____   Boy._____

This type of musical analysis is very helpful in understanding the rhythm of the song and the breakdown of the song into musical phrases. This information is necessary for the actor to determine the best places to breathe so as not to interrupt the musical phrase in inappropriate places. The air passages, in particular, often serve as transition points in the communication of the message of the song. For the director, these air passages serve as ideal places for movement. In the air passages, when the singer is not singing, it is easier to focus on movement. Since the air passages frequently are transition moments, movement in these places is also helpful in underscoring the emotional content of the song.

Figure 7. YANKEE DOODLE DANDY (Warner Brothers, 1942). James Cagney as George M. Cohan in his exciting rendition of the title song. Cohan agreed to the movie only if Cagney played the role. Cagney, who was a song and dance man in his early days, jumped at the opportunity. His enthusiastic performance along with Michael Curtain's superb direction won Cagney an Oscar and made this one of the all time most popular films.

Assignment 3
Reciting the Lyric

Select a song of a different type from another musical presented in the class oral reports. Speak, without musical accompaniment, the lyric of the song, incorporating all of the elements from Assignment 2. Include the rhythms of the song as you recite; clap or tap the rhythm of the vamp, air, and rideouts.

Assignment 3
Grading Sheet

Evaluation of Musical Acting Project _____

Student _____ Date _____

Title of Selection _____

Authors/Composers_____

Evaluation Scale: 4 Excellent
                        3 Very Good
                        2 Good
                        1 Fair

Comments	Specific Ratings	Score
	Choice	
	Consistency of rhythm	
	Understanding of musical phrasing	
	Poise	
	Analysis of musical material	
	Grade	Total

Further Remarks:

_____

_____

_____

_____

_____

Figure 8. Ray Bolger, one of the theatre's best loved dancing stars here in Richard Rodger's ON YOUR TOES.

Chapter Three

MUSICAL MOVEMENT: ESTABLISHMENT OF CHARACTER THROUGH MOVEMENT

Before examining the movement demands of the character and the libretto, the musical theatre actor needs a kinesthetic awareness of his own body as well as the energy requirements of the role he will physicalize. The following is a list of some physical techniques which are necessary to achieve the kinesthetic awareness:

1. There must be a commitment on the part of the actor to each and every gesture. A move half done is better not done at all.

2. Gesture is a physical punctuation and enhancement to the text. Movement needs to support the phrasing in the text for maximum effectiveness.

3. Body positions have to be open enough to the audience so that the actor can be seen and heard clearly.

4. In standing, weight should be distributed evenly between both feet, with the upstage foot slightly ahead of the downstage foot. In initiating a cross (including entrances) beginning with the upstage foot looks infinitely less awkward and, in fact, is easier to accomplish.

5. In general, gestures should be executed with the upstage arm because it leaves the body open and appears less awkward. The same applies to kneeling on one knee. Kneeling on the downstage knee looks less awkward and leaves the body open.

6. When sharing a scene the actor needs to be on the same plane with his acting partner. If he is even slightly downstage of the partner, he is upstaging himself. If he is even slightly upstage of the partner, he is upstaging the partner.

7. Simultaneous movement is humorous.

8. Don't move on a laugh line. Moving splits the focus and interrupts the laugh. Don't continue movement until the laughter has reached its peak and begins to subside.

9. An actor should move on his own line rather than on

someone else's line unless he is supposed to be the focal point of the audience.

10. When turning on stage, turn keeping the body open to the audience. The actor should not cross over his own feet in the turn.

11. An actor should be aware of his own idiosyncrasies and posture as an individual so that he can keep gestures that are distinctively personal from inappropriately intruding on the physicality of the character.

12. An actor may need to "counter" a move either stage right or stage left to balance the stage picture if someone crosses in front of him.

13. Movement of the eyes has the potential of either detracting from or enhancing the focal point of the audience. By looking at someone the actor gives focus to that person. This focus is strengthened if additionally the body turns in the same direction as the head and eyes.

14. Wear clothing and shoes during the rehearsal process that simulate as nearly as possible the clothing and shoes to be worn in performance. These things greatly affect movement patterns as well as the ability to execute movement.

15. Use the props as early as possible in the rehearsal period. The use of props affects the timing of gesture as well as the delivery of lines.

16. The actor must get the script out of his hands as soon as possible. The body cannot be used constructively until it is unhampered by the presence of the script. Holding the script also gives the actor a false sense of body usage and he often is not aware of when his hands will be free. This can cause movement problems later in the rehearsal period.

17. One of the biggest problems for an actor is the use of energy. An actor must first become aware of his own habitual energy and then determine the habitual energy of the character. Control of energy is crucial so that it is neither too high nor too low. The control of energy level is also important because of the multiple levels of communication in performance. The presence of the audience requires an energy level that is heightened above the everyday use of the body. Energy is a factor in making gestures large enough to communicate intended messages to the audience. Energy is also affected by the physical space in the theatre. A larger space requires a greater extension of energy than a smaller space. In all cases an actor's ability to control his energy is crucial not only for believability from the audience's perspective, but also for the safety of his fellow actors. This is imperative in scenes where extensive physical

Figure 9. RUMPELSTILTSKIN, *A Players U.S.A.—WONDRAWHOPPER— written and directed by William-Alan Landes. Note the character stance of Rumpelstiltskin. (Left to Right) Rumpelstiltskin (Don Agey), Serina (Marjorie E. Clapper) and the King (Terry Vreeland).*

movement or violence occur. The actor must learn to give sufficient movement stimulus to achieve the desired response, but not so much stimulus that there is the potential of hurting himself or his partners on stage.

18. In analyzing the play, the actor needs to determine the climax of the play as a whole, as well as the crises moments for the individual scenes. These are important in body usage and gesture. Just as an opera soprano only has one or two high C's during the course of an evening's performance, to be truly effective an actor needs to know where in the play he is angriest or happiest or saddest so he builds to those moments and doesn't diffuse his energy for them too early in the play. One of the things that holds the audience's attention is potential—the potential of the character struggling for control. If an actor shouts through the entire play, the shouting loses its effectiveness. If the character jumps up and down every time he gets angry, this too loses effectiveness. Once the actor has shown the audience the limits of his movement and energy, he can do no more. The high C of the soprano is more effective if the audience thinks she can also sing a high D than if they are painfully aware that the C is absolutely her top note.

19. It is important for the actor to warm up physically as well as vocally before the rehearsal period to make maximum use of the time allotted. This warm-up should result in a state of relaxed tension. While this may at first sound contradictory, the actor must in fact be sufficiently relaxed so that the body can do what is natural for the character (and indeed natural for any human being). However, he must also be in a state of readiness to work. This same relaxed tension is required for performance because of the necessity of communicating to the audience.

20. Any movement reflective of a period of time other than the actor's own requires in-depth, separate analysis and more rehearsal time for the actor to feel confident and comfortable with the specific demands of the clothing and manners of that day.

Basic to any physical projection of character is correct posture and an understanding of weight distribution. Any physical adjustments of the body to express particular characters emanate from a **neutral-energetic posture**. Relaxation is essential to such a posture. However, the relaxation is active rather than passive, signifying a readiness to begin movement. In establishing this posture, the following exercises have proved helpful. Slowly lower the body forward with head down, bending at the waist, arms hanging loosely, fingers touching the floor. Release all tension through the fingers, loosely shake the arms. Roll the body upwards to a standing position, imagining the vertebrae are blocks and you are carefully stacking them one on top of the other until you reach your full height. The head is the final body part to be put into position. The actor might also do the exercise thinking of the spinal column as an open zipper that is closing while the body is rolling upwards. In addition, the image of a string attached to the crown of the head running through the center of the body will help the actor maintain proper body alignment.

NEUTRAL ENERGY CHECKLIST

A checklist for the actor to verify neutral energetic posture would include the following:

1. Crown of the head is highest part of the body.
2. Head in easy swiveling position.
3. Chin is level (parallel to the floor), never raised.
4. Back of neck extended upward.
5. Front of neck always loose, never stretched.
6. Shoulders back and relaxed down.
7. The image of the shoulders reaching to the horizons is a helpful one.
8. Overall chest cavity expanded; sternum lifted.
9. Hands fall a bit in front of the thighs. No tension in arms.
10. Thighs forward and loose.
12. Knees released, not locked in place. Calf muscles loose.
13. Body resting lightly on both sides of feet and all toes. Weight evenly distributed between both feet. Feet should be hips width apart.
14. Body adjusts to character stance and movement **FROM** above.

Along with a Neutral Energetic Posture, an actor needs to have correct body alignment. This alignment includes the ears in place over the shoulders, the shoulders in place over rib cage, the rib cage in place over the hips, the hips in place over the knees, and the knees in place over the ankles. This alignment of the body encourages the maximum elongation of the spine while retaining the three natural curves of the spine. (See Chart.) In this way, the actor can better balance his weight and maintain a clear center for his body weight. It will be easier to move from this posture and alignment than it would be from a body position that is neither centered nor balanced. This Neutural Energetic Posture and body alignment is also helpful in eliminating unnecessary tension from the body.

FIGURE 10.   *An actor demonstrates neutral energetic position.*

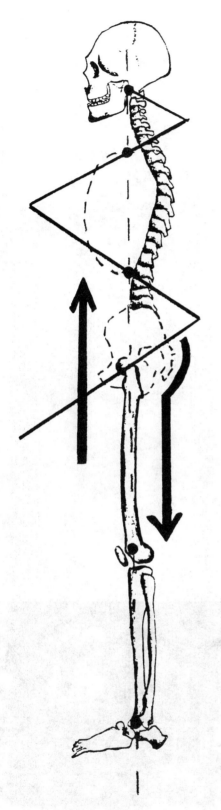

Figure 11. BODY ALIGNMENT CHART.
Three Curves of Spine in Proportion.

When moving the student should imagine his feet in strong contact with the floor, providing a solid base for his weight. However, rather than letting the floor be responsible for the weight, the actor should take control of his own weight. By thinking of his weight as moving up and away from the floor as the feet remain in strong contact with the floor, the actor can achieve a sense of "lightness" in his movements, as well as a greater ease in moving.

When developing the physicality of a character, one of the first things which the actor may change is placement of the center of the weight for the character so that it differs from the actor's personal center. The actor will notice that as the center is changed, the altitude of gestures will change as well. There may be additional vocal quality changes that accompany the choice of where to place the character's center of weight. By experimenting with different centers of weight, the actor has a multitude of possibilities for the physicalization of many characters.

Physical Attitudes for Musical Characters

Once the actor has established the posture, it is important to remember that all movement emanates from the center of the body rather than any one limb. Movement that is expressive of any character needs to involve the body as a whole with all parts in unity to express a single message. An analysis of character attitude, gestures and movement must be specific in order to be useful for the actor. The following lists are by no means complete, but offer the actor specific possibilities for movement and attitude choices. The actor should not limit himself to one attitudinal choice. During the rehearsal period, he should explore as many possibilities as he can, ultimately discarding those which are inappropriate and using those he finds helpful. The actor should feel free to add his own perceptions to the lists.

Rational: Explanatory, instructive, didactic, admonitory, condemnatory, indignant, puzzled, curious, wistful, pensive, thoughtful, preoccupied, deliberate, studied, candid, guileless, thoughtless, innocent, frank, sincere, questioning, uncertain, doubting, incredulous, critical, cynical, insinuating, persuading, coaxing, pleading, persuasive, argumentative, oracular.

Pleasure: Peaceful, satisfied, contented, happy, cheerful, pleasant, bright, sprightly, joyful, playful, jubilant, elated, enraptured.

Pain: Worried, uneasy, troubled, disappointed, regretful, vexed, annoyed, bored, disgusted, miserable, cheerless, mournful, sorrowful, sad, dismal, melancholy, plaintive, fretful, querulous, irritable, sore, sour, sulky, sullen, bitter, crushed, pathetic, tragical.

Passion: Nervous, hysterical, impulsive, impetuous, reckless, desperate, frantic, wild, fierce, furious, savage, enraged, angry, hungry, greedy, jealous, insane.

Self-Control: Calm, quiet, solemn, serious, serene, simple, mild, gentle, temperate, imperturbable, nonchalant, cool, wary, cautious.

Friendship: Cordial, sociable, gracious, kindly, sympathetic, compassionate, forgiving, pitying, indulgent, tolerant, comforting, soothing, tender, loving, caressing, solicitous, accommodating, approving, helpful, obliging, courteous, polite, confiding, trusting.

Antagonism: Sharp, severe, cutting, hateful, unsocial, spiteful, harsh, boorish, pitiless, disparaging, derisive, scornful, satiric, insolent, insulting, impudent, belittling, contemptuous, accusing, reproving, scolding, suspicious.

Comedy: Facetious, comic, ironic, satiric, amused, mocking, playful, humorous, hilarious, uproarious.

Energy: Lively, eager, excited, earnest, energetic, vigorous, hearty, ardent, passionate, rapturous, ecstatic, feverish, inspired, exalted, breathless, hasty, brisk, crisp, hopeful.

Apathy: Inert, sluggish, languid, dispassionate, dull, colorless, indifferent, stoical, resigned, defeated, helpless, hopeless, dry, monotonous, vacant, feeble, dreaming, bored, blasé, sophisticated.

Self-importance: Impressive, profound, proud, dignified, imperious, confident, egotistical, peremptory, bombastic, sententious, arrogant, pompous, stiff, boastful, exultant, insolent, domineering, flippant, saucy, positive, resolute, haughty, condescending, challenging, bold, defiant, contemptuous, assured, knowing, cocksure.

Timidity: Meek, shy, humble, docile, ashamed, modest, timid, unpretentious, respectful, apologetic, devout, reverent, servile, obse-

Figure 12. OKLAHOMA ! Jekyll Island Musical Theatre Festival. Note the lively energy and playful comic attitude of the characters of Ado Annie and Will Parker.

quious, groveling, contrite, obedient, willing, sycophantic, fawning, ingratiating, deprecatory, submissive, frightened, surprised, horrified, aghast, astonished, alarmed, fearful, terrified, trembling, wondering, awed, astounded, shocked, uncomprehending.

In order to analyze the specific movement required for the character you are attempting to express, the following terms will be helpful. The actor should explore as many possibilities as seem appropriate for the character.

Specific Movement Terms For Musical Characters

(A reminder to be precise and explicit in describing character movements.)

1. Ambling	31. Freezing	61. Reeling	91. Staggering
2. Ascending	32. Galloping	62. Rescuing	92. Stalking
3. Awakening	33. Gambling	63. Revolving	93. Standing
4. Balancing	34. Giggling	64. Retrieving	94. Streaking
5. Bouncing	35. Gliding	65. Rolling	95. Stretching
6. Bounding	36. Grooving	66. Rubbing	96. Surveying
7. Bowing	37. Groping	67. Sashaying	97. Swaying
8. Careening	38. Grunting	68. Sauntering	98. Swerving
9. Cavorting	39. Heaving	69. Scampering	99. Swishing
10. Circling	40. Hobbling	70. Schlumping	100. Tapping
11. Clapping	41. Hopping	71. Sculpturing	101. Tipping
12. Closing	42. Hovering	72. Searching	102. Tossing
13. Clumping	43. Hustling	73. Secluding	103. Tracking
14. Conducting	44. Jiving	74. Shimmering	104. Trembling
15. Contorting	45. Jogging	75. Shrinking	105. Tumbling
16. Crawling	46. Jumping	76. Shuffling	106. Turning
17. Creeping	47. Kissing	77. Skating	107. Twisting
18. Crouching	48. Leaping	78. Skipping	108. Uprearing
19. Daring	49. Lifting	79. Slamming	109. Walking
20. Daubing	50. Loosening	80. Sliding	110. Washing
21. Descending	51. Lunging	81. Slinking	111. Wasting
22. Destroying	52. Lurching	82. Slipping	112. Watching
23. Dipping	53. Opening	83. Slithering	113. Waving
24. Diving	54. Painting	84. Slouching	114. Whirling
25. Drooping	55. Perching	85. Slumming	115. Wiggling
26. Dwelling	56. Plodding	86. Smashing	116. Wrenching
27. Dying	57. Plunging	87. Spinning	117. Writhing
28. Embracing	58. Pouncing	88. Sprawling	118. Yawning
29. Flexing	59. Preening	89. Spreading	
30. Flopping	60. Primping	90. Springing	

Movement Preparation

Musical theatre makes more demands on the movement requirements of an actor than the non-musical theatre. While the style and period of a non-musical affect the type of movement an actor chooses, the style and period of a musical are heightened, creating an enlarged atmosphere. In this larger than life sphere, set, costumes, and props are often exaggerated in color and size. This requires, in many cases, that an actor use a broader movement pattern. In addition, since the energetic force of the orchestra, and, often, a stage full of chorus members, can easily dominate an actor's performance, the musical performer needs to sustain a high level of energy and to release it and expand it when required. A great deal of physical stamina is obviously required for singing and dancing, but the musical actor must remember that a consistently high level of energy is required for the total performance. Too many musical performances become virtually lifeless once the dialogue starts after a musical interlude. Anyone interested in musical theatre acting must participate in dance and movement classes on a regular and continuing basis so that the actor can increase stamina and technical abilities, as well as recognize the level of energy required to convey a musical performance.

As movement preparation, a performer should begin with a series of exercises necessary to warm up the body and initiate the flow of energy. There are many fine exercises that can be used to accomplish a good warm up. The following list is suggested as one suitable preparation for classwork or performance.

Warm-Up Exercises for the Body
1. Do the exercises to establish correct posture as already noted.
2. Circle the head right, back, left, and forward. Repeat three times. Reverse the movement.
3. Look to the right, tucking chin in. Hold left shoulder down with right hand. Hold 5 slow counts. Look to the left, hold right shoulder down with left hand, hold 5 slow counts. Repeat.
4. Roll the right shoulder from back to front 5 times.
Roll the left shoulder from back to front 5 times.
Roll the right shoulder from front to back 5 times.
Roll the left shoulder from front to back 5 times.
Repeat the whole exercise alternating shoulders.
Repeat using both shoulders simultaneously.
5. Yawn, and while yawning, interlock fingers with palms facing away from body and stretch arms forward, rounding shoulders, then stretch arms overhead, shoulders down, fingers still locked, release

FIGURE 13.   Actors demonstrate exercise #3 to release shoulder tension.   Valdosta State University.

FIGURE 14.   Actors demonstrate initial position for the Yawn Stretch, exercise #5.   Valdosta State University.

hands overhead and stretch arms behind you as they return to your sides. Repeat.

6. Do a figure eight with the right arm. Repeat three times. Do a figure eight with the left arm. Repeat three times. Do figure eights using both arms simultaneously, letting them cross in front of you. Repeat three times.

7. Extend arms straight in front of body. Shake hands to wrists, hands to elbows, hands to shoulders, shake shoulders to pelvis, shake pelvis to knees, shake knees to ankles. Balance on right leg and shake left foot. Balance on left leg and shake right foot.

8. Jog in place to a slow count of 24, pumping the arms vigorously as you move.

Gesture

Once the character's attitudes and basic movement patterns have been chosen, the actor then works to develop appropriate gestures which express the character. This is especially important when an actor is singing. So often competent actors who can convey characters through movement in any scene are exceedingly uncomfortable when using their hands and arms during the rendition of a song. The musical theatre actor should assume a neutral arm position while singing with the elbows comfortably away from the body, thereby minimizing tension in the arms and hands and allowing for a greater freedom and fluidity of arm movement.

There are two general categories of gestures: **Overt gestures** are wide, expansive gestures which flow from the center of the body outward and **covert gestures** are minimized gestures which are positioned close to the performer though still originating at the center of the body. **Gestures** are the punctuation marks of physical characterization, and as such need a clear beginning, middle, and end. Each individual gesture should be clearly and cleanly finished before another gesture begins to avoid slurring of movement.

Gestures have the following purposes:

1. To emphasize
2. To illustrate
3. To imitate
4. To indicate.

An **emphatic gesture** supports the text and serves as an exclamation point. An **illustrative gesture** pantomimes emotion, facts, or a demonstration. An **imitative gesture** copies or mimics. An **indicative gesture** points out a direction. (Sometimes the term **indicative gesture** applies only to gestures pointing away from a performer, while **autistic** refers to gestures which indicate the actor

FIGURE 15. Example of Illustrative Gesture. Character is asking for money.

FIGURE 16. Example of Indicative Gesture. Character is pointing out a direction.

himself.)

Gestures may also be categorized by qualities.
1. Altitude
2. Flow
3. Integration
4. Strength
5. Tempo

Altitude refers to the height of the gesture. **Flow** suggests the movement of the gesture into, away from, or across the body. **Integration** associates something in the environment to the actor. This quality of a gesture refers to the use of props, set pieces and costumes by an actor, as well as the tactile communication between actors. **Strength** refers to whether a gesture is forceful or weak. **Tempo** refers to the speed of a gesture; whether a gesture is fast or slow. While any gesture may combine all or several of the above qualities, one quality should be clearly prevalent.

Figure 17. JACQUE BREL IS ALIVE AND WELL AND LIVING IN PARIS, *Players U.S.A. Notice forceful gesture with high altitude of character on the left. Christine Avila (Left), Avril Chown (Right). Produced by William-Alan Landes.*

In order to analyze the specific movement required for a character, the following form will be helpful.

MOVEMENT ANALYSIS CHART I

The following form poses questions which will be helpful to the actor or director when making movement choices for specific characters. These questions are directly related to information about the character which is found in the libretto or in the lyrics of the score. This form would best be filled out as the libretto or score are being read with specific notations from the text used in the blank spaces.

For example, temperature and time of day make a difference in movement. In *CAMELOT*, the "Lusty Month of May" takes places outdoors at a lunchtime picnic in the spring when the weather is neither hot nor cold. The spring feeling suggests free, open, easy movement in contrast to the more rigid "court" movement of some later scenes. References in the script to "Flower gathering" suggest the use of flowers as props. The month of May and the medieval time period suggest, for the director, the possible inclusion of a may pole. The long skirts for women in the medieval period suggest the need for rehearsal skirts.

Examples of "necessary movement" would include entrances, exits, drinking of wine (i.e. Arthur invites Guenevere and Lancelot to "drink a toast" with him), and a page enters with a rose and a note for Guenevere.

What does the libretto request as necessary movement or business which identifies or must be incorporated into the character?

_____

_____

_____

How do the sets, furnishings, props and costumes affect movement and business; how can they be used to enhance characterization?

_____

_____

_____

What does the physical climate/environment and familiarity with surroundings suggest about character movement? Do these change the movement in some scenes?

_____

_____

_____

How is movement affected by age, status, education, and health?

_____

_____

_____

How does the time period of the musical affect the movement?

_____

_____

_____

How does the musical show type affect the movement?

_____

_____

_____

Vocal Warm-Up Exercises

It is important for the singer to be vocally warmed up before any singing is done. The first step in this process should be to eliminate any unnecessary tension from jaw, neck or shoulders. This can be accomplished through the following exercises:

1.   **Yawning:** Yawning is an excellent technique for reducing tension. When yawning, however, do not pull the lips back against the teeth. Try to maintain a more forward, neutral, easy lip position.
2.   **Swallowing:** Swallowing is another excellent technique for reducing muscular tension in the upper body. The action of swallowing releases neck and jaw muscles while at the same time lubricating the vocal folds.
3.   **Stretching:** Stretching is a very useful technique for reducing tension in jaw, neck and shoulders. This can be accomplished by rotating the head to the right, back, left and forward, and then reversing the sequence to the left, back, right and forward. Next the shoulders can be rotated forward and back, both singly and together. Make sure when rotating the shoulders that the movement is isolated, focusing on the shoulder area without involving full body movement. Execute the shoulder rotation slowly and thoughtfully, stretching the shoulder forward, up to the ear, back and down and then reverse the direction of the rotation. Refer to Chapter 2 and the warm-up exercises for the body for a suggested sequence for the head and shoulder movements.
4.   **Shaking:** The last technique for reducing unnecessary upper body tension is shaking the muscles. Start by shaking hands, then shake the arm up to the elbow, then shake the entire arm. While continuing to shake the arms, add shaking of one leg then the other leg, then hip area and finally the head. In the final stages of this exercise, vary the level at which the arms are shaking, moving them from a high position to a low position and from one side to the other side.

The second step in the vocal warm up process is to warm up the vocal folds. There are three exercises to help accomplish this goal.

1.   **Humming:** This is a very non-stressful means of beginning to warm up and of maintaining relaxation in the vocal folds.

The hum can be done on any comfortable pitch or while changing pitches. If the rest of the body feels unnecessarily tense, shaking the muscles while humming can help to reduce tension. The shaking need not be as vigorous while humming as it was when done in the previous step.

2.   Sighing: The action of sighing works best when accompanying a yawn. Yawning in this stage of the warm up has a different purpose than the yawning in the previous step. Initiate a yawn. When the yawn is at the most open point, initiate an easy sigh from a high pitch to a low pitch.

3.   Vowel Sounds and Humming: Initiate a hum on a low pitch and move slowly to a higher pitch. On reaching the highest pitch desired, begin the vowel sound and continue to a lower pitch. Open vowel sounds such as "mo," "maw," and "mah" work well to maintain the relaxation in jaw and neck areas. This exercise is <u>not</u> to be done with a piano. The actual pitches are not important. The goal of the exercise is to maintain a free and easy movement from a low pitch to a high pitch and back to a low pitch.

The third step in the vocal warm up is formal vocalization, This would include scales and exercises specifically appropriate for the singer's vocal range and abilities. These exercises vary considerably from singer to singer and vocal coach to vocal coach.

Figure 18. PETER N'THE WOLF. *A Players U.S.A. WONDRAWHOPPER. Book, Lyrics and Directed by William-Alan Landes. Music by Gary Castillo. The Cat (Marjorie E. Clapper), projects her personality.*

MOVEMENT ANALYSIS CHART II
(Personal Movement)

Before physicalizing a character, it is necessary to be aware of personal movement patterns. The following form will help you do this.

My name is _____

How old am I? _____   What do I think of my age? _____
_____

How does my body posture express my age, health, and inner feeling? _____
_____

What is my weight? _____   What do I think of it? _____
_____

Where is my weight centered? _____

Where does tension reside in my body? (Headaches, neck or shoulder tension, lower backaches, etc.) ____
_____

Do I have any physical limitations which hamper my movements? _____
_____

Do I have any mannerisms? (Include any vocal as well as physical; cracking knuckles, rubbing nose, clicking

teeth, smacking gum, etc.) _____
_____
_____

What do I think of them? _____
_____

How do I sit, stand, and walk? _____
_____
_____

Are my basic movement patterns jerky or smooth, strong or light, quick or slow, direct or indirect? (Circle one in each category.)

What animal image might suggest my basic movement patterns? (i.e. koala bear, peacock, etc.) _____
_____

Assignment 4

Using the selection from Assignment 3, while speaking the lyric and maintaining the rhythm of the song, walk in rhythm with the meter of the song. Repeat the exercise walking against the rhythm of the song.

Assignment 4
Grading Sheet

Evaluation of Musical Acting Project _____

Student_____Date_____

Title of Selection _____

Authors/Composers _____

Evaluation Scale: 4 Excellent
                      3 Very Good
                      2 Good
                      1 Fair

Comments	**Specific Ratings**	**Score**
	Movement in rhythm w/song	
	Movement against rhythm of song	
	Consistency of rhythm	
	Understanding of musical phrasing	
	Poise	

Grade   Total

Further Remarks:

_____

_____

_____

_____

Assignment 5

Using the movement analysis chart presented on page 36, analyze the movement for a musical character of your choice. Select a song that you will perform in character without the use of the lyrics. Attempt to express the sentiment of the lyric as well as the essential movement patterns of the character. Present the movement of the character during the song without singing the lyrics.

For example, in *CAMELOT*, immediately preceding the song "How To Handle a Woman" a rose has been left on stage by Guenevere. During the course of the song the actor might pick up the rose, which becomes for him the character of Guenevere. He then holds the rose tenderly, sings to the rose and, possibly, kisses the rose lightly at the conclusion of the song when he has reached the decision to "love her." Additionally the character is in a state of agitation as the song begins. The movement pattern should be quicker and the amount of movement greater in the first half of the song. The actor or director should remember, however, that though this is one possible interpretation for the song it is not the only interpretation. Let your imagination lead you from your responses to the form.

Sample Movement Analysis Chart

Sample Song: "When Frederic Was A Little Lad" *Pirates of Penzance*. Ruth.

What does the libretto request as necessary movement or business which identifies or must be incorporated into the character?
Exits "in despair"; Passed by pirates from Frederic to Pirate King in Scene 1; Is present when the pirates sing opening song; Uses a pistol; Enjoys laughter with King & Frederic.

How do the sets, furnishings, props and costumes affect movement and business; how can they be used to enhance characterization?
The use of the pistol would be particularly helpful in suggesting more masculine movement patterns. She seems like "one of the boys" though she loves Frederic.

What does the physical climate/environment and familiarity with surroundings suggest about character movement? Do these change the movement in some scenes?
Just left a pirate ship;
Rocky seashore on the coast of Cornwall — setting suggests explorative movements and climbing. Ruined chapel by moonlight might suggest furtive movements.

How is movement affected by age, status, education, and health?
Nurserymaid; not afraid of work; calls herself stupid; hard of hearing; mistook "pilot" & "Pirate"; Middle aged; gray hair; vows revenge.

How does the time period of the musical affect the movement?
The late 19th Century would suggest long full skirts, possibly boots for the feet.

How does the musical show type affect the movement?
PIRATES OF PENZANCE is an operetta with little emphasis on dialogue; Character motivation is much like musical comedy. The Character of Ruth will rely in part on the charm of the actress.

WHEN FREDERIC WAS A LITTLE LAD

W. S. Gilbert

Arthur Sullivan

some ca-reer sea - far - ing. I_ was, a - las! his nurs-'ry-maid, and
be - ing hard of hear - ing. Mis - tak - ing my in - struc-tions, which with-
break it to my mas - ter. A_ nurs-'ry-maid is_ not a - fraid of_

so it fell to *my* lot, To take and bind the_
in my brain did gy - rate, I took and bound this_
what you peo - ple *call* work, So I made up my mind to_

prom-is-ing boy ap - pren-tice to a *pi - lot*. A
prom-is-ing boy ap - pren-tice to a *pi - rate*. A
go as a kind of pi - rat-i-cal maid-of - all-work. And

life not bad for a har-dy lad, though sure - ly not a high lot, Though
sad mis-take it_ was to make, and doom him to a vile lot, I
that is how you find me now, a_ mem-ber of your shy lot, Which you

I'm   a   nurse, you might do   worse than make your boy a   pi - lot!
bound   him to   a   pi - rate - you! - in - stead of   to   a   pi - lot!
would-n't have found, had he been bound ap - pren - tice to   a   pi - lot!

After 3rd verse

Notes on Movement Choices based on the Movement Analysis Chart I:

Factors from the complete chart which might affect movement in the song are:
1.   Within the lyrics Ruth claims to be hard of hearing.
2.   Ruth is at least 47 years old and has gray hair.
3.   Ruth uses a pistol.
4.   Ruth is the only woman on a pirate ship and calls herself a "pirate maid of all work."

The fact that Ruth is hard of hearing might cause her to walk leading with her head, straining to hear. The fact that she uses a pistol and has been around men for a long time would suggest a strong walk with large steps, perhaps standing with feet wide apart and hands planted firmly on hips. Though sometimes interested in appearing feminine, she would be awkward when doing so. Because the show type is an operetta, all movement might be larger than life. The specific lyric of the song tells of Ruth's mistake. By the end of the song Ruth has resolved to make the best of her error. She seeks to convince the pirates of the truth of her tale. Ruth's movements might be described as daring and sprawling. Her attitude might be described as explanatory, curious, and cheerful.

Assignment 5
Grading Sheet

Evaluation of Musical Acting Project _____

Student _____ Date _____

Title of Selection _____

Authors/Composers _____

Evaluation Scale: 4 Excellent
                       3 Very Good
                       2 Good
                       1 Fair

Comments   **Specific Ratings**   **Score**

                                Choice of material
                                Analysis of character
                                Appropriateness of gesture: quality
                                                                    purpose
                                Clarity of gesture: quality
                                                              purpose
                                Establishment of character attitude
                                Establishment of character movement pattern
                                Involvement of total body in movement pattern
                                Appropriate energy level expressed
                                Appropriate energy level sustained

                                Grade   Total

Further Remarks:

_____

_____

_____

_____

_____

_____

Chapter Four

ACTING THE SONG

A good musical theatre actor makes the audience feel that his song is created while it is being sung, that the song never existed until the situation motivated him to sing. The singer also must suggest from moment to moment in the song that he is conveying a message large enough to be musical. A well sung song sounds like an ad lib. The greatest difficulty for the actor lies in sustaining this spontaneity through a prolonged musical phrase, or while attempting to hold a high C.

This seeming spontaneity is the result of careful analysis which begins, for the musical performer, with an examination of the music. Mark any vocal music to identify vamp, verse, chorus, air, and rideout. Also, identify any musical passages which pose specific difficulties for you as a singer. You need to be aware that standard sheet music may differ considerably from the arrangement of the song in the original score. These differences may appear in changes of key and time signature, altering of note values, and editing out of verses and interludes. Lyrics may also be changed because of vulgarity or personal preference. Thus, the relationship of the song to character and plot may be considerably altered.

It is likewise important for the musical theatre actor to perceive the song in relation to the musical as a whole. The meaning of the song out of context may be altered. For example, out of context, "Everything's Coming Up Roses" from *Gypsy* sounds like a very upbeat, up tempo, positive rhythm song. However, within the context of the musical, it is a ballad in which the character undergoes emotional transitions which may include moving from hurt to anger to desperation to resolve. In addition, the song serves as the climactic moment of the first act.

In addition to an analysis of the music, the musical theatre actor must analyze the lyric. The term **subtext**, the meaning behind

Figure 19.   Cole Porter's RED, HOT AND BLUE. *Bob Hope's last appearance on Broadway. Jimmy Durante and Ethel Merman are also in this routine.*

the words, applies to musical as well as nonmusical acting, and is necessary in any analysis of lyrics as well as dialogue. Song lyrics may be divided into four categories:

1. Narrative
2. Didactic
3. Subjective
4. Communicative

A **narrative lyric** tells a story ("Surrey With the Fringe on Top"). A **didactic lyric** instructs ("The Farmer and the Cowman Should Be Friends") or gives personal information about the character ("I'm Just a Girl Who Cain't Say No"). A **subjective lyric** involves the audience with the character's emotions or personal difficulties ("Many a New Day"). A **communicative lyric** is one designed to excite the audience and involve it in the energy of the moment ("Oklahoma!").

Once the music and lyrics have been analyzed, the musical theatre actor can begin to articulate the **subtext**, the meaning beneath the lyrics, and to answer the following questions:

What is the character's objective (goal) in singing the song?

How does that objective relate to the character's super-objective (ultimate goal) in the show?

Does the character make significant comments about other characters or relationships with other characters in the song?

What does the libretto indicate about the presentation of the song?

What is the character's age at the time of the song?

What is the character's health at the time of the song?

What is the character's environment at the time of the song?

What is the character's social status at the time of the song?

What is the character's educational background at the time of the song?

What is the character's occupation at the time of the song?

What is the character's clothing at the time of the song?

Do any of the above differ from one song to another by the same character?

What is the character's dominant attitude in the song?

What other attitudes are present in the song?

Are any of the attitudes conflicting?

Is the attitude at the beginning of the song the same as the attitude at the end of the song? If the attitude has changed, articulate the change that occurs.

In order to answer these questions, the musical actor must use the same mental tools as the nonmusical actor: (1) observation; (2) recall; (3) imagination. **Observation** is the ability to perceive those

Figure 20. JACK N'THE BEANSTALK, *a Players U.S.A.* WONDRAWHOPPER *written and directed by William-Alan Landes. The Giant (Terry Vreeland) and Beanseller (Joseph W. Witt). Comic acting for a song. Jack (Tom Cicero) has his back to us.*

specific elements which differentiate the actions of one person from another by studying people in the actions of their daily lives and at their emotional extremes. **Recall** is the process by which the actor draws on personal experiences identical to or similar to the character he is portraying. **Imagination** is the mental ability to project oneself into a different personality and a different locality. The use of imagination allows for a wider spectrum of characterization by not limiting the actor to choices which are totally self-related. Through the use of imagination the actor is able to integrate his mental tools with his physical tools of voice and body. The ultimate goal for the musical theatre actor is to delineate a character clearly through the coordinated use of physical and mental tools, despite the distractions to concentration which continually occur for the actor in musical productions.

Necessarily, musicals make large demands on the actor's powers of concentration. **Concentration** is the ability to ignore all distractions and focus attention on the immediate requirements of the role.

In order to develop the skill of **observation** the musical theatre actor should spend 15 minutes a day observing the activities of those around him, seeking to identify the idiosyncrasies that differentiate one person from another, and noting how a person's behavior may differ from situation to situation. The observed should vary in age, ethnic background, social status, and occupation as the actor seeks to broaden his range of experience and extend the possibilities of his character choices. It is suggested that these observations be noted in a journal which may be used as a reference tool for the development of character.

In developing the skill of **recall**, the journal may also be used. It is helpful to remember some turning point or intense moment from your past and write down in as much detail as possible what **actions** you did at that time. These notations may also be a useful tool for later character development. Additionally, as the musical theatre actor analyzes the lyrics of a song, look for emotions or situations in the song that are similar to situations or emotions you have experienced personally. In recalling these emotions or situations be as specific as you can in relation to actions and gestures which you employed at the time. It is also helpful to recall any sense responses to the experience: sounds, colors, smells, textures, or tastes associated with the memory. In this way it is possible to create very believable characters within the musical framework when required.

The skill of **concentration** can be developed through the following exercises:

Figure 21. Julie Andrews during rehearsal. She exhibits the necessity of concentration during the rehearsal process.

1. Breathing exercise: Inhale to a count of 5, hold the air for a count of 5, and exhale to a count of 5. As the respiration process occurs, focus your attention on the action of the diaphragm muscle as it controls both the hold and exhalation phases of the exercise. Increase the count to 6, 7, 8, or 9 to extend both concentration and breath control.

2. The class sits in a circle clapping either a 4/4 rhythm or a 3/4 rhythm. Once the rhythm is established, each member thinks of the title of a musical. Starting at any point in the circle, one person names this musical in rhythm. Each subsequent person in the circle adds his musical while naming all previous musicals and continuing to maintain the established rhythm. Naming continues as many times around the circle as members can recall. If a participant forgets a musical or distorts the rhythm, he must leave the circle. For variety the same exercise could be done with song titles, composers, or musical theatre actors.

Now the musical theatre actor is ready to analyze the phrasing of the lyrics. A musical phrase, like a dialogue phrase, is a unit of thought. The delivery of the lyric is made more difficult by the musical accompaniment. The actor may be limited by his ability to control the respiration process. Careful attention needs to be given to the marking of breaths so that the actor is comfortable and the musical phrase is not compromised. Obviously, interrupting words for breathing is inappropriate and interferes with the message transmission of the lyric. The actor should carefully practice the most effective places to breathe within the lyric before marking them. Once marked, the actor needs to practice taking the breaths as marked so they become second nature. The following exercises will contribute to the development of phrasing and breath control:

1. Singing the letters of the alphabet on a single tone breathe first after each 8 letters: ABCDEFGH//IJKLMNOP//QRSTUVWXYZ

2. Then singing the letters of the alphabet on a single tone, breathe after the first 12 letters: ABCDEFGHIJKL//MNOPQRSTUVWXYZ

3. Then, finally, sing the letters of the alphabet on a single tone in a single breath.

4. The breathing exercise discussed earlier can also be used to develop breath control. Add the element of exhaling a sound, using "f," "s,", or "ah."

Be careful to maintain a steady breath stream on the exhalation. Avoid allowing excess air to escape at the initiation of the exhalation.

Assignment 6

Select a lyric and write it out in your own handwriting. Underline each subject once and each verb twice in the text to help the actor perceive the series of thoughts expressed within the lyric, apart from the musical accompaniment. Once the thoughts are determined, mark appropriate breathing places with the (^) symbol. Careful attention should be paid to the air portions of the music. Rehearse with an accompanist and present the song, focusing on the breathing process. On the right, in Sample Assignment 6, subjects have been underlined once, verbs have been underlined twice, and breaths have been indicated on the music for *GIVE MY REGARDS TO BROADWAY*.

Assignment 6
Grading Sheet

Evaluation of Musical Acting Project_____

Student _____ Date _____

Title of Selection_____

Authors/Composers _____

Evaluation Scale: 4 Excellent
                        3 Very Good
                        2 Good
                        1 Fair

Comments	**Specific Ratings**	**Score**
	Choice of material	
	Appropriate subject/verb markings	
	Appropriate breath marks:	
	too many?	
	too few?	
	Ability to control the breath through	
	the musical phrase	
	Vocal quality	

                    Grade   Total

Further Remarks:

_____
_____
_____

Sample Assignment 6

GIVE MY REGARDS TO BROADWAY

George M. Cohan

Figure 22. LITTLE JOHNNY JONES. George M. Cohan early in his career bridging the gap from Vaudeville to Broadway Musical.

Figure 23.   I'D RATHER BE RIGHT.   George M. Cohan at the end of his career, a greatly beloved and honored showman.

start for Old New York once more? _____ With
smile and charge it up to me; _____ Men-tion

tear - dimmed eye they say good - - bye, they're friends with
my name ev - 'ry place you go, as 'round the

out a doubt; _____ When the man on the pier
town you roam; _____ Wish you'd call on my gal, Now re -

Shouts,"Let them clear," as the ship strikes out. _____
mem - ber, old pal, when you get back home. _____

Whis - per of how I'm yearn - - ing, To min - gle with the old time throng,_____ Give my re - gards to old Broad - way and say that I'll be there e'er long._____ long._____

Extra! Extra!

Note: The series of thoughts underlined indicate the strong use of verbs with the implied subject "You." The song is a command on the part of the solo singer to the chorus. The objective might be to convince the chorus to give the solo singer's regards to Broadway. The number should be performed with a very high energy level.

Assignment 7

Using the song from Assignment 5 or choosing a new song, analyze the lyrics according to **purpose**, note any particular situations or emotions you can identify within the lyrics, mark the phrases within the lyrics for breath, establish character movement and gestures. Present the song, speaking the lyric naturally rather than rhythmically. However, sustain pauses created by vamp, air, and rideout. The actor needs to fill these pauses with appropriate character subtext and movements.

Assignment 7
Grading Sheet

Evaluation of Musical Acting Project _____

Student _____ Date _____

Title of Selection _____

Authors/Composers _____

Evaluation Scale: 4 Excellent
                        3 Very Good
                        2 Good
                        1 Fair

Comments	**Specific Ratings**	**Score**
	Choice of Material*	
	Characterization:	
	a. clarity of attitude	
	b. appropriateness of gesture	
	c. suitability of movement	
	d. sustaining of character	
	Analysis of lyric:	
	a. purpose	
	b. clarity of subtext	
	Use of pauses	
	Appropriate breath marks	

the instructor may suggest a change of selection

                        Grade   Total

Further Remarks:

_____

_____

_____

Assignment 8

Rehearse your song selection from Assignment 7, adding the musical accompaniment, and present it.

Grading Sheet

Evaluation of Musical Acting Project _____

Student _____ Date _____

Title of Selection _____

Authors/Composers _____

Evaluation Scale: 4 Excellent
                      3 Very Good
                      2 Good
                      1 Fair

Comments	**Specific Ratings**	**Score**
	Choice	
	Characterization:	
	a. clarity of attitude	
	b. appropriateness of gesture	
	c. suitability of movement	
	d. sustaining of character	
	Use of pauses	
	Appropriate breath marks	
	Musical expertise:	
	a. interpretation of song rhythm	
	b. pitch	
	c. vocal quality	
	Appropriate energy	

                      Grade   Total

Further Remarks:

_____

_____

_____

_____

Figure 24. (Above.) Paula rehearses her dance numbers at full energy; projecting her character and acting the dance as she would her dialogue or song. Note the bright mood she projects.

Figure 25. (Right.) A dance performer must act the character throughout the dance number. Compare the difference in mood and tone projected in both Plates on this page.

Chapter Five

ACTING THE DANCE

A good musical theatre actor not only makes the audience feel that he is creating the song while it is being sung, but also that he is creating the dance as it is being performed. The dance, like the song, must seem an ad lib. The continuing difficulty for the actor is to sustain the spontaneity through a series of movement patterns which require both agility and kinesthetic awareness.

Musical theatre acting requires the development and maintenance of basic dance skills in the areas of ballet and jazz. In addition, classes in social dance forms (including the waltz, Latin American dances, jitterbug, Charleston, etc.), tap, and acrobatics are highly desirable. In order to maintain flexibility and agility, the actor needs to take classes on a continuing basis. Unfortunately, one of the actor's basic tools, his body, is only as good as it is today. What the actor could do yesterday or last year is of little value in meeting the physical requirements of the character he is creating today. Hopefully, his movement skills will develop, and he will have more flexibility and agility as time goes on, rather than less. Good health is basic to the maintenance of physical skills. Proper diet and adequate rest will pay large dividends to the far-sighted actor.

Since musical theatre makes higher demands on a performer's level of energy than non-musical theatre, the actor should be aware of the necessity of maintaining sufficiently high energy. The following questions may help the actor to determine a stronger kinesthetic sense in regard to his own energy level.

1. Are my warm ups sufficient to energize my body for the demands of the production?

2. Am I increasing my energy sufficiently to logically lead into solo or production numbers, or is there an abrupt change in energy exertion when the music begins? Ideally, the character should have a throughline of energy which makes the musical number the natural

A. *Minimal Energy*

B. *Moderate Energy*

C.
Maximum
Energy

Figure 26.   Levels of energy.

outcome of the dialogue which immediately precedes it.

3.   Am I maintaining my energy level following musical numbers, or is there an abrupt drop? It is, in fact, necessary to **increase** the energy level following a musical number since the actor no longer has the benefit of musical accompaniment and/or choral support which the number provided.

4.   Am I maintaining my energy level while executing choreography? If an actor finds it necessary to concentrate on the mechanics of specific movement patterns and specific counts, the throughline of energy will be interrupted.

5.   Do I check before each of my entrances to see if I am maintaining my throughline of energy? There are often lengthy time periods separating entrances, and energy can easily dissipate in backstage activity.

The actor uses these movement skills and energy levels to master the dance patterns created for the production by the choreographer. He also uses his analytic skills to project the thoughts behind those patterns. Most dances in contemporary musicals move the show and the character logically forward or expose some hitherto unseen element of a character. They may also reflect the mood of the production or the character, as well as production style and period. Since many dances are created utilizing specific set pieces (i.e. levels, stairs), specific props (i.e. umbrellas, beach balls), or specific costumes (i.e. capes, hats), the actor must develop an expertise that goes beyond the simple memorization of steps.

In analyzing the patterns created by the choreographer, the actor should discover the purpose which the dance accomplishes. The following are the most common purposes of dance numbers in contemporary musicals: to cause an entrance, to cause an exit, to make a discovery, to make a decision, to comment on society, to comment on self, to establish or develop conflict, to remember the past, to clarify the present, or to foretell the future. Not all dances accomplish these purposes. Many simply exist to show the virtuosity or special skills of the performers who created the roles. Some examples include Gwen Verdon in *Sweet Charity*, Ann Miller's tap dancing in *Sugar Babies*, or the ensemble performers in *A Chorus Line* or *Cats*. In addition, there are shows which require special skills (*42nd Street*'s tap routines, *Barnum*'s circus routines). Many choreographers are delighted to discover special skills (juggling, gymnastics, mime, etc.) which an actor may have developed and to incorporate them into production or solo numbers.

One of the actor's primary responsibilities in dancing a song is his ability to work well with the choreographer. He must begin with the mastery of steps, which requires concentration during rehearsal, and, often, extra hours in individual practice away from company rehearsals. He must demonstrate a willingness to meet all reasonable choreographic demands. He must be physically and mentally prepared to start dance rehearsals, having warmed up his body and his enthusiasm, as well. (The exercises in preceding chapters may be useful in achieving this preparation.)

Figure 27. "Mastering the steps." Extra hours of individual rehearsal and practice. Bob Fosse and Gwen Verdon dancing.

These statements pertain to performances in leading roles, but a vast majority of beginners will find themselves relegated to chorus work. The chorus is an ideal opportunity to develop the skills necessary for leading performances. In musicals, the dance required of chorus members is often more demanding than that of principal performers. In chorus work, the primary responsibility of the actor is to execute movement patterns identically with his fellow chorus members. The purpose of the actor is to blend into the ensemble, rather than to appear as an individual, and to provide focus, rather than to take focus.

Figure 28. CHORUS LINE, New York Shakespeare Festival. Directed by Michael Bennett with book by James Kirkwood and Nicholas Dante, music by Marvin Hamlisch, lyrics by Edward Kleban and produced by Joseph Papp. (Left to Right) Sammy Williams, Pamela Blair, Donna McKechnie, Robert LuPone, Carole Bishop and Priscilla Lopez.

All musical actors, when developing the dance and movement patterns of the choreographer, will find it imperative to work in front of a mirror, observing and correcting posture, gesture, attitude, and the technical requirements of movement. In this way the actor can correct his mistakes and enhance his kinesthetic awareness away from the tension and interaction of full rehearsals.

In approaching the dance elements of a musical theatre role, the actor needs to perceive the emotional content of the dance just as he perceives the emotional content of the song or the scene. By making a commitment to this emotional content, the actor will enhance his energy level and also enable himself to move beyond the mere execution of steps to the more compelling performance and communication of the emotional message of the dance sequence.

Chapter Four assignments are based on using the following choreographic pattern. If a choreographer is available to the class, any other series of 32 counts may be substituted.

	1-4	4 Walks Downstage (R-L-R-L)
"Chaine turn"	5-8	Walking turn to the R (R-L-R-L)
"Lindy"	9-10	Side together Side (R-L-R)
	11-12	Ball, Change (L-R)
"Chaine turn"	13-16	Walking turn to the L (L-R-L-R)
	17-20	4X Step Brush hop
		17 Step L, Brush R Heel, hop L
		18 Step R, Brush L Heel, hop R
		19 Step L, Brush R Heel, hop L
		20 Step R, Brush L Heel, hop R
"Lindy"	21-22	Side together Side (L-R-L)
	23-24	Ball, Change (R-L)
	25-28	Walk in a circle to the R (R-L-R-L)
"Soutenue turn"	29-30	X R over L
		Full turn - L
		(Execute turn on balls of feet)
Jump to 2nd	31	jump, land on both feet (feet should be hips width apart)
Jump to 1st	32	jump feet together and parallel

As the actor works with this choreographic pattern for Assignments 9—11, it is imperative to review the material in Chapter Three dealing with Neutral Energetic Posture and Alignment. The weight of the actor needs to be centered, the spine elongated and the body correctly aligned for the proper execution of not only this choreographic sequence, but any choreographic sequence.

Figure 29.   HELLO, DOLLY! Courtesy of the Shubert Theatre Organization. Billy Daniels (Horace Vandergelder) and Pearl Bailey (Dolly Gallagher Levi).

Assignment 9

In order to develop a keener sense of energy exertion, execute the 32 counts of choreography in the following manners:

1. Do the 32 counts with minimal energy extended by the actor. Make no attempt to slow down the rhythm of the movement.

2. Do the 32 counts with moderate energy extended by the actor.

3. Do the 32 counts with maximum energy extended by the actor. Make no attempt to speed up the rhythm of the movement.

Note: If the actor has difficulty achieving maximum energy, the movement sequence may be executed twice as fast as what was previously done. However, it is important to then repeat the above exercise working toward maximum energy extension without the necessity of speeding up the rhythm pattern. It would be beneficial to videotape this exercise so students could see the body working at three different energy levels.

For those performers with habitually low energy levels, several things can be done to increase their energy level.

1. Before performing with the maximum energy, the actor should jog around the theatre or performance space several times to increase the heart rate and the flow of oxygen to the brain. The actor should then be aware of greater energy in the performance of the exercise. (A simple, but not always as effective, form of this is running-in-place.)

2. On a personal kinesthetic level, if the actor is someone with a low enery level, it should feel "overdone" when working at the maximum energy level. It should not feel like the normal extension of energy for the performer.

3. Actors may find shaking the muscles helps to increase energy level. Begin by shaking hands, then shake hands and lower arm to elbow, then shake the full arm, add shaking the legs and finally add shaking the head.

4. The single factor which will help the actor most is a clear commitment to the movement and the use of the total body in executing the movement.

Assignment 9
Student Worksheet

Answer the following questions about yourself.

1.   During minimal extension of energy:
   1.   What was my posture?

   _____

   2.   Did I have a tendency to slow down or speed up the movement?

   _____

   3.   Was the overall feeling of the movement light or heavy?

   _____

II.   During moderate extension of energy:
   1.   What was my posture?

   _____

   2.   Did I have a tendency to slow down or speed up the movement?

   _____

   3.   Was the overall feeling of the movement light or heavy?

   _____

III.   During maximum extension of energy:
   1.   What was my posture?

   _____

   2.   Did I have a tendency to slow down or speed up the movement?

   _____

   3.   Was the overall feeling of the movement light or heavy?

   _____

IV.   Which of these three energy levels is closest to my own?
   a.   As a person _____

   b.   As a performer _____

V.   During the execution of all three of these levels of energy, were all the parts of my body moving at
        the same level? If not, which part of the body seems least able to maintain the maximum energy?

   _____

   _____

   _____

   _____

Assignment 9A
Student Worksheet

Answer the following while observing a classmate executing Assignment #9. When this form is completed, compare it with your partners. Discuss the similarities and the differences for the class.

I. During minimal extension of energy:
1. What was his/her posture?

_____

2. Was there a tendency to slow down or speed up the movement?

_____

3. Was the overall feeling of the movement light or heavy?

_____

II. During moderate extension of energy:
1. What was his/her posture?

_____

2. Was there have a tendency to slow down or speed up the movement?

_____

3. Was the overall feeling of the movement light or heavy?

_____

III. During maximum extension of energy:
1. What was his/her posture?

_____

2. Was there a tendency to slow down or speed up the movement?

_____

3. Was the overall feeling of the movement light or heavy?

_____

IV. During the execution of all three of these levels of energy, were all the parts of the body moving at the same level? If not, which part of the body seems least able to maintain the maximum energy?

_____

_____

_____

_____

_____

_____

Assignment 10

Choose three appropriate contrasting characters from among the following. Perform the 32 count sequence expressing the physical characteristics of each. Use a costume piece for each which would affect movement (i.e. long skirts, boots, suit, high heeled shoes).

List One — Female Characters

Annie Oakley, *Annie Get Your Gun*
Eliza Doolittle, *My Fair Lady*
Auntie Mame, *Mame*
Sarah Brown, *Guys and Dolls*
Polly, *The Boyfriend*
Mrs. Lovett, *Sweeney Todd*

List Two — Male Characters

Don Quixote, *Man of LaMancha*
Billy Bigelow, *Carousel*
Huck Finn, *Big River*
Daddy Warbucks, *Annie*
Rolf, *Sound of Music*
Caliph, *Kismet*
King, *King and I*

Identify three adjectives from the lists in Chapter 2 that describe the movement for each of the three characters.

Character 1: _____
_____
_____

Character 2: _____
_____

Character 3: _____
_____
_____

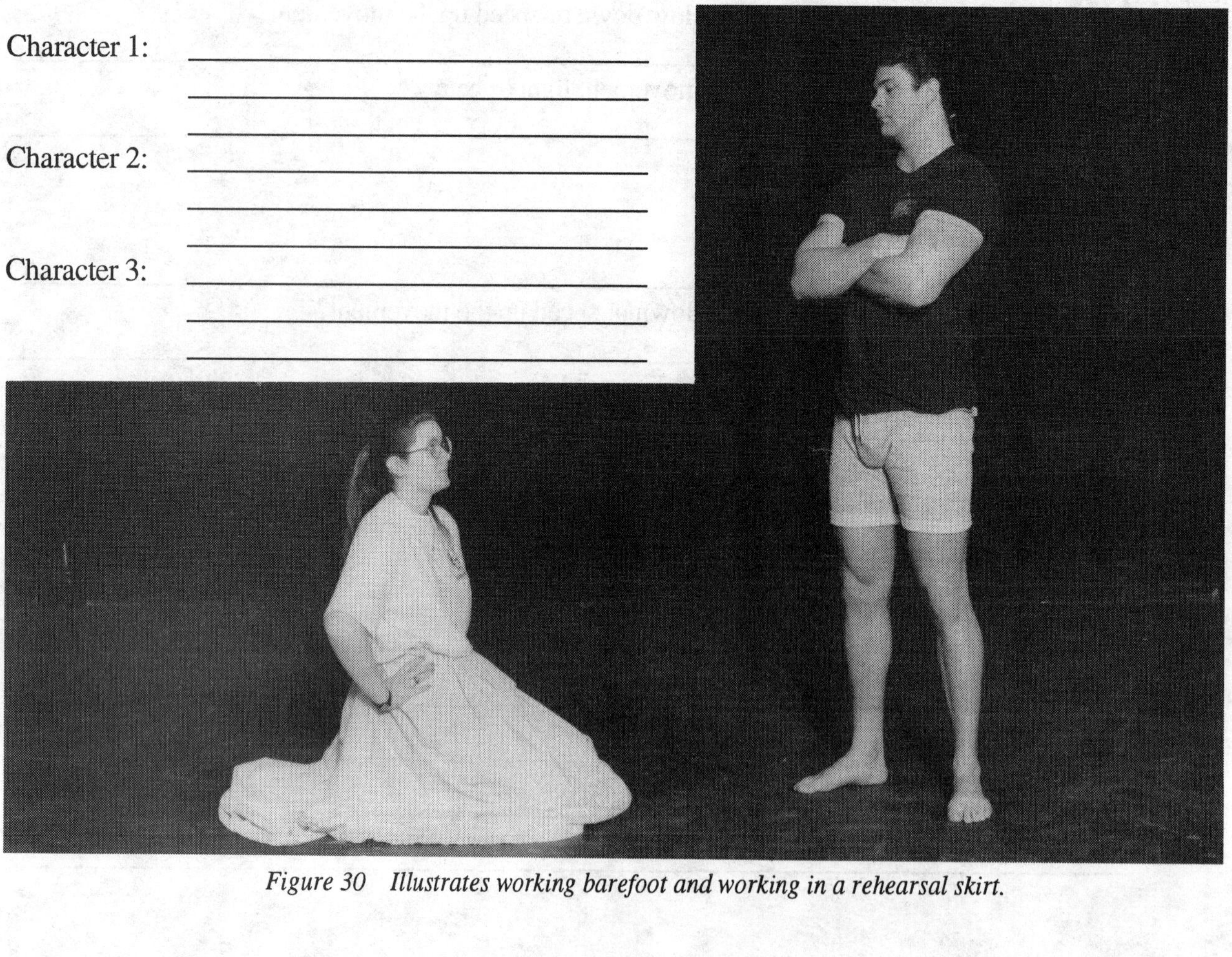

Figure 30   Illustrates working barefoot and working in a rehearsal skirt.

Assignment 10
Grading Sheet

Evaluation of Musical Acting Project _____

Student _____ Date _____

Evaluation Scale: 4 Excellent
                     3 Very Good
                     2 Good
                     1 Fair

Comments	**Specific Grading**	**Score**
	1. Appropriate energy:	
	a. Character 1	
	b. Character 2	
	c. Character 3	
	2. Adjustment of movement to suggest character:	
	a. Character 1	
	b. Character 2	
	c. Character 3	
	3. Appropriateness of adjectives chosen:	
	a. Character 1	
	b. Character 2	
	c. Character 3	
	4. Use of costume piece	
	a. Character 1	
	b. Character 2	
	c. Character 3	

Grade   Total

Further Remarks:

_____

_____

_____

Figure 31.   Lions

Figure 32.   Sailors

Figure 33.   Tramps and Sailors

Assignment 11

Divide the class into groups of three or more. Have each group perform the 32 count sequence as three different groups of characters. Choose from among the following or create your own groups of characters.

Sailors	Lions	Musketeers	Ghosts
Gangsters	Cats	Socialites	Delinquents
Gypsies	Dogs	Tramps	Pirates
Children	Werewolves	Farmers	Orientals
Cowboys	Vampires	Clowns	Cossacks

Grading Sheet

Evaluation of Musical Acting Project _____

Group Members_____

Date _____

Evaluation Scale: 4 Excellent
                      3 Very Good
                      2 Good
                      1 Fair

Comments	Specific Grading	Score
	Appropriate energy	
	a. Set 1	
	b. Set 2	
	c. Set 3	
	Unification of movement	
	a. Set 1	
	b. Set 2	
	c. Set 3	
	Unified projection of appropriate attitude:	
	a. Set 1	
	b. Set 2	
	c. Set 3	

           Grade   Total

Further Remarks:

_____

_____

_____

Figure 34.   KISS ME KATE.   The Megaw Theatre.

Chapter Six

MAKING MUSICAL COMEDY COMIC

Acting in Musical Comedy demands analytical expertise. While careful analysis of the script is expected, classic musical comedies (those preceding *Oklahoma!*) baffle contemporary musical actors. They are logical in neither script construction nor in character development. Consequently, musical comedy actors often have to supply logic and motivation that they find missing in the libretto and score. In an analysis of the script, two early considerations are the date of the original production and the names of the stars and featured performers in the original production. Musical comedy is quite often based on topical issues. It is essential that the actor be aware of those topical issues which affect the comedy in order to project the character intended in the libretto and score. The actor, likewise, needs to be aware of the original stars and featured performers of the roles which were usually written with these specific individuals in mind. The roles are often dependent on a certain personality type, embodied by the original actor. If a musical actor cannot suggest some of the elements of the original personality type, then the actor must substitute new qualities that will give substance to an otherwise underwritten role.

As well, some characters have no function in the development of the plot but are simply on hand to offer the actors who played them an opportunity to do solo turns of the type with which an audience associated them. It is difficult for today's actors to play these characters who have neither logical motivations nor integration into the script. An actor playing one of these roles must recognize that the role itself is a stereotype, and, rather than being limited by such an assignment, must bring to the role aspects of his own personality which will enhance the role. The actor needs, also, to use his own personal charm, charisma and warmth to distract the audience from recognizing the limitations of the role.

The stock characters, simple dialogue, and conventional plot of the classical Musical Comedies such as *Anything Goes* will not prove limiting to an actor who has faith in his own personality and in his own ability to recognize standard comic devices., Comic devices are of many types. Some of the most common are: **derision**, in which humor stems from poking fun at physical needs (*Annie Get Your Gun*), status (*Unsinkable Molly Brown*), or the revelation of hidden flaws (*Sweet Charity*); **incongruity**, which juxtaposes objects, situations, or people which are obviously different (*My Fair Lady*) or places characters in totally different surroundings (*Mame*) or places the real in conflict with the ideal (*Guys and Dolls*); **automatism**, in which humor stems from lost human flexibility (*Once Upon a Mattress*) or behavior so oft repeated that it becomes mechanical (*Where's Charley*); **humors**, in which the humor stems from some imbalance or excess in character (*Bye Bye Birdie*). In contemporary musical comedies these comic devices are not mutually exclusive. While the classic Musical Comedies [those musical comedies written before 1943] are simplistic in their use of standard comic devices, most contemporary Musical Comedies [those musical comedies written after 1943] use combinations of or all of the standard comic devices (*Hello, Dolly!*)

Librettos which are identified as "musical comedy" fall into three different categories which are dependent on the cause of the humor in the text. In **traditional musical comedy,** the humor lies in stereotypical, easily recognizable character types and illogical plot development which always resolves itself happily and generally with the boy getting the girl. In **musical farce**, broader physical action is added to stereotypical characters. Plot action generally is quicker in the musical farce than in traditional musical comedies. In **high musical comedy**, the dominant humorous element resides in the language of the text and the lyrics.

Musical Farces have no message and no intellectual appeal. They rely on physical movement, gags, tricks, exaggerated set and costume designs, and stock situations, such as mistaken identity (*Funny Thing Happened on the Way to the Forum*). In Musical Farce, the actor needs to recognize that plot and character are simple, stereotypical, and clarified early in the libretto. The actor needs to analyze the libretto and ascertain how soon and effectively he must establish his character and his character's contribution to plot development. Once these have been defined, the actor needs to analyze the movement requirements of the libretto and score

Because of the broadened physicality of farce, the actor will need to focus much of his attention on the kind of movement which

Plate 3. CABARET, *Arte Johnson stars as the Emcee with Belle Calaway also starring as Sally Bowles. Courtesy of Long Beach Civic Light Opera. Photo by Craig Schwartz.*

delineates his character type. Often included in Musical Farce are chases and fights. A great deal of physical exertion is required.

High Musical Comedy places greater emphasis on dialogue and lyrics which may make use of word play, puns, insults and oddity in word choice and word arrangement. It deals with established and recognizable codes of behavior and morals (*PAL JOEY*). Such musicals are easier for the actor to analyze as their construction and dialogue are close to their nonmusical counterparts. The actor, however, needs to be aware that in High Musical Comedy lyrics must be closely analyzed since they more often serve to develop plot and character than in Classic Musical Comedy and Farce Musical Comedy. The emphasis on the language of the text requires that the actor focus much of his attention on his vocal abilities. Variety in pitch, rate, and volume become especially important in handling the verbal word play of the High Musical Comedy adroitly.

Contemporary Musical Comedy (those musical comedies written after 1943) is less stereotypical than Traditional Musical Comedy. The production of *OKLAHOMA*! serves as a turning point in the development of this genre. Rodgers and Hammerstein developed the **Integrated Musical** in which libretto and score are logically related in a cause and effect pattern. The element of dance is integrated in the libretto and score as well. There is less reliance on the personality of the actor and more emphasis on the creation of individual characters in the libretto. Some of the songs in this form take on the same qualities as monologues that are found in nonmusical scripts (i.e. "Lonely Room" from *OKLAHOMA!*). The characters presented in the Integrated Musicals of Contemporary Musical Comedy prepared the way for the stronger emotional content and multi-dimensional characters of the Musical Drama.

The comedy element in Contemporary Musical Comedy is frequently strongest in the supporting characters of the libretto rather than in the major characters. Ado Annie and Will Parker are good examples of the use of humor in secondary characters. The comic development of their relationship parallels the more serious development of the relationship between Curly and Laurie. There is also humor in the even lesser characters of Gertie and her Peddler.

Contemporary Musical Comedy uses recognizable humorous elements from all of the Traditional Musical Comedy forms including Musical Farce and High Musical Comedy. When approaching comic characters in Contemporary Musical Comedy, the actor needs to explore all the comic possibilities of Traditional Musical Comedy and make specific choices about which are the most applicable. The comedy of the character of Ado Annie relies on the

Plate 4. ANNIE, *John Schuck as Daddy Warbucks, Marcia Lewis as Miss Hannigan and Krista Leonard as Annie. Courtesy of the Long Beach Convention and Entertainment Center. Photo by Craig Schwartz.*

comic device of HUMORS. She sings of her excess in character when she admits she "Cain't Say No." There is also the element of physical action from Musical Farce when Ado Annie becomes so jealous of Gertie that she chases her and ultimately pulls Gertie's skirt over her head.

In all types of musical comedy, it is necessary for the actor to be aware of the technique of timing. Careful timing and control is necessary in the performance of any physical humor. Remembering that movement can serve as a punctuation to the text will enhance both comic value and clarity. Simultaneous movement is another example of comic timing. Verbal timing is a third example of comic timing. The actor must be aware of his punch lines so he can deliver them without rushing. Many a laugh has been lost because an actor's rate of speaking was too fast or too inarticulate. Timing a punch line also depends on the actor's awareness of laughter in the audience so he can wait for the laughter to subside before he continues to speak.

The assignments which follow encourage the actor to explore the comic devices found in Traditional Musical Comedy, Musical Farce and High Musical Comedy. By understanding the humor in these forms, the actor will be better able to understand and project humor in whatever musical genre it appears.

Assignment 12

Choose a Classical or Contemporary Musical Comedy from the following list or select one of your own. Select from it a scene, five to ten minutes in length, for three or more performers with dialogue which leads to a group song. Determine the stereotype of the character and the comic device employed in the humor. Note references in the libretto and score which support your choices. Present the scene for evaluation.

CLASSIC	CONTEMPORARY
Good News	*Me and Juliet*
Of Thee I Sing	*Barnum*
Over Here	*Oklahoma!*
Something's Afoot	*Company*

To aid students in the completion of this assignment, fill out the student worksheet on page 75. It is best to complete the worksheet as the actor reads the libretto and score so that specific notations from the text can be used in the blank spaces. For more interesting characters, some choices might include a combination of stereotypes or the addition of an adjective with the stereotype. For example, instead of "young lover" the actress might choose "bumbling fool," or add the adjective "proud" to "young lover." Always the choices need to be relative to textual references but in classic musical comedy the text leaves much room for choices. Playing these characters can then become more interesting for the actor and more entertaining for the audience. The inquisitive actor might review the stock characters found in 16th century Commedia dell'arte scenarios (i.e. "Pantalone" — crochety old man, "Arlecchino" — mischievous servant, etc.)

Assignment 12
Student Worksheet

Name_____ Date_____

Character_____

Musical Comedy_____

Specific character references in the libretto

_____

_____

_____

_____

_____

Specific character references in the score

_____

_____

_____

_____

_____

Character stereotype (one word)_____

Comic device(s) employed_____

_____

_____

_____

_____

Actor's personality traits which are appropriate to developing the character

_____

_____

Assignment 12 Sample Scene   **LEAVE IT TO JANE**

The following scene and worksheet are presented as a sample for the student. The worksheet on page 81 has been completed using direct quotations, where applicable, from the scene and lyrics included here. The scene includes three characters and moves from the dialogue into the presentation of the title song of the musical.

BESSIE.   Another scalp for Jane.
JANE.   Nonsense.
BESSIE.   Did you see the way he looked at her?
STUB.   The thing I want to know is why Jane told that poor young man a deliberate fib. *(Crossing BESSIE to R. C.)* Jane, why did you say old Bolton was there — *(Points off.)* When he is really there — *(Points to house.)* ...talking to your father?
JANE.   He mustn't meet father yet.
BESSIE.   Why not?
STUB.   There's a glitter in her eye, Bessie! *(He moves close to Bessie.)* I believe she's plotting something.
BESSIE.   *(Crossing to Jane.)* Jane! Have you thought of any way to prevent that all-American half-back from going to Bingham?
JANE.   I've thought of a way it might be done.
STUB.   Great! Kiss her for me, Bessie — kiss her!

(BESSIE stops him.)

JANE.   No, it may not work. There's so little time — besides — it isn't a very nice thing for a girl to do.
BESSIE.   You're going to flirt with Mr. Bolton?
JANE.   I'm afraid I'll have to...a little. *(Crossing to L C.)*
BESSIE.   I see — you'll lead him on — and make him think he has a chance to win out if he sticks on here at Atwater?
STUB.   He's crazy about you already. If ever I saw a case of love at first sight. Oh Lady — Lady — *(JANE goes up. STUBBY thinking of WITHERSPOON goes over L. Crossing Jane.)* But will Prexy admit him?
JANE.   No, that's the difficulty. Listen. *(He comes to her.)* Of course father knows Mr. Bolton is crazy to have his son go to Bingham.
STUB.   Well then...
JANE.   That's why father must never know young Mr. Bolton **is** young Mr. Bolton.
BESSIE.   *(Coming to R of Jane.)* But what are you going to do?
JANE.   I'm going to try to get Mr. Bolton to change his name.
BESSIE.   Jane, you're a a marvel.
STUB.   Bessie, you said it. There is none like her, none.

LEAVE IT TO JANE (TRIO: BESSIE, JANE, STUB)
(All sitting on fountain.)

LEAVE IT TO JANE

Words by
P. G. Wodehouse

Music by
Jerome Kern

Plate 5. Kathleen Murray, seated, left, listens to Dorothy Greener admonish Angelo Mango in the 1959-60 Off-Broadway revival of Leave It To Jane *at the Sheridan Square Playhouse.*

Assignment 12
Student Worksheet

Name_____Date_____

Character_____Jane_____

Musical Comedy_____Leave It To Jane_____

Specific character references in the libretto
_____"Jane...told a fib"_____
_____"There's a glitter in her eye."_____
_____"She's plotting something"_____
_____Jane says she's going to flirt._____
_____
_____

Specific character references in the score
_____"She is the girl with a brain"_____
_____Jane will "get you out of it [trouble]"_____
_____Jane always knew "the right thing to do"_____
_____"Her tact and sense were simply immense"_____
_____"She'll tackle [problems] gaily, a score or more daily"___

Character stereotype (one word)_____Coquette_____

Comic device(s) employed   _Mistaken identity; Jane also takes on some of the qualities of the scheming servant from the commedia dell 'arte. She plots and schemes and flirts._____
_____

Actor's personality traits which are appropriate to developing the character
_____Possible traits might include mischievous, strong sense of humor, energetic, and friendly.___
_____

Assignment 13

In preparation for Assignment 13, the student should complete the worksheet on page 83. Once the choices for movement and attitude have been made the actor can begin to physicalize the character. The choices physically should be as bold as possible since farce is so dependent on physical action. The form should be completed as the score and libretto are read so that specific notations can be used to fill the blanks. The third adjectives will be the hardest to choose but the addition of the third adjective will greatly enhance the creative possibilities for the actor. This form should not limit the imagination. It should rather serve to extend the imagination. It is a "jumping off" place for the creation of the character not the "finishing line."

Choose a Musical Farce from the following list or choose one of your own. Select from it a scene five to ten minutes in length for three or more performers with dialogue which leads to a group song. Movement in the scene and song should reflect the attitudes and movements chosen. Review the lists of Physical Attitudes and Specific Movements from Chapter Two. Choose those which best delineate the characters in the scene, then present the scene for evaluation.

Once Upon a Mattress
Funny Thing Happened on the Way to the Forum
The Boyfriend
Your Own Thing
Dames at Sea
Boys from Syracuse

Suggestions by Instructor:

_____

_____

_____

_____

_____

_____

_____

_____

_____

_____

Assignment 13
Student Worksheet

Name _____ Date _____

Character _____

Musical Farce _____

Analysis of Character _____

_____

_____

Classification of song _____

3 adjectives describing physical attitudes

_____

_____

_____

3 adjectives describing movement

_____

_____

_____

Comments by Instructor:

_____

_____

_____

_____

_____

_____

_____

Assignment 13
Sample Student Worksheet

Name _____ Date _____

Character _____ Lou Ellen _____

Musical Farce _____ *Oh Boy!* _____

Analysis of Character _____ Lou Ellen is the steady, stable character of reason at the center of a collection of delightfully eccentric characters. Lou Ellen's superobjective is to keep the man she loves and has just married. She attempts to convince the girls that old fashioned ideas of marriage are the best.

Classification of song _____ Charm song _____

3 adjectives describing physical attitudes

_____ nervous _____
_____ joyful _____
_____ enraptured _____

3 adjectives describing movement

_____ creeping _____
_____ gliding _____
_____ shimmering _____

Comments by Instructor:

_____
_____
_____
_____
_____

Assignment 13 Sample Scene   **OH BOY!**

Notes on Preparing the Sample Scene:

The song is a charm song which partially depends on the personality of the actress playing Lou Ellen. In rehearsing this sample scene, some of the specific areas for the actress to focus on would include answering the following questions:

What do I do when I am nervous?

What do I do when I am joyful?

What do i do when I am enraptured?

Can I remember a time in my life when I experienced a sense of nervousness similar to what the director and I perceive Lou Ellen feels in this scene? What are some of the sense images which come to mind concerning this experience?

Can I remember a time in my own life when I experienced a sense of joy similar to what the director and I perceive the character of Lou Ellen feels in this scene? What are some of the sense images which come to mind concerning this experience?

By answering these questions, appropriate gestures and movements can be chosen and more easily sustained through the presentation of the song. Energy can be more appropriate when the actress makes a more personal commitment to the emotional content of the song.

POLLY. What a shame?

JANE. Spoiling our party.

(The GIRLS are looking out of the wiondow. One holds her hand outside, she pantomimes, but the rain is falling on it.)

POLLY. Just when we'd got the food ready!

GIRLS. (At window.) Oh, look, it's started raining.

(They are chattering together with their backs to the bedroom door, when LOU ELLEN peeps out. She tries to steal to door unobserved, but they see her as she reaches it. She carries her hat and cloak.)

POLLY. (Crossing to stop her.) Why, who's the little girl? (With JANE, she drags her C. one on each side of her. GIRLS gather around her, leaving L. window open.)

LOU ELLEN. Oh...excuse me...

JANE. Have you come to the party?

LOU ELLEN. Y...yes.

POLLY. (R of LOU ELLEN.) Well, you're too late. I'm afraid it's over.

LOU ELLEN. (Starts for door again.) Then I guess I may as well go home.

POLLY. Oh, no, we'll go to the Cherrywood Inn Cabaret as soon as Mr. Marvin comes back.

LOU ELLEN. Oh, I...I never go to cabarets.

JANE. (L of LOU ELLEN.) No, why not?

LOU ELLEN. My...my husband wouldn't like it.

POLLY. You're married?

LOU ELLEN. Y...yes, I'm married.

JANE. Well, bear up, don't let it make you morbid.

POLLY. Love, honor and be gay is the vow the modern wife takes.

LOU ELLEN. But I'm an old-fashioned wife. I promised to obey my husband.

(Music cue: Start introduction of IN THE GOOD OLD-FASHIONED WAY.)

POLLY and JANE. How perfectly foolish. (Exit JANE and POLLY R. 2. E.)

(One GIRL puts lights out at switch on post L.C. and ALL GIRLS get cushions on introduction of number. LOU ELLEN gets small rocking chair from behind curtain L. C. and brings it down C.)

AN OLD FASHIONED WIFE

Words by
P.G. Wodehouse

Poco allegretto e grazioso

Music by
Jerome Kern

1. The mod—ern wife leads a dread—ful life, That seems the mod—ern fash—ion._____ For wick—ed ways And cab—a—
2. It's thought quite queer if they last a year, These mar—riag—es that we know._____ You've hard—ly cried; "Here comes the

bey,_____ From my home___ I'll nev — er stray._____ Al –
day,_____ Till our two heads are bent and gray._____ Through

though the thing that's smart, is_____ To be out all night at
days se — rene and storm–y_____ There will be but one man

par –ties,_____ I'll be sit–ting_____ With my knit–ting_____ In the
for me,_____ And we'll weath–er_____ Life to geth—er_____ In the

1
good old fash — ioned way._____
good old fash — ioned way._____

2
way.
way._____

(Exit ALL. After number, exit GIRLS. LOU ELLEN exits into bedroom.)

Figure 35. An original poster.

Assignment 13
Grading Sheet

Evaluation of Musical Acting Project _____

Students _____ Date _____

Title of Musical _____

Title of Song _____

Authors/Composers _____

Evaluation scale: 4 Excellent
                         3 Very Good
                         2 Good
                         1 Fair

Comments   **Specific Ratings**   **Score**

                         Choice
                         Characterization:

                             a.   Clarity of attitudes
                             b.   Appropriateness of movements
                             c.   Sustaining of movements
                                     through song
                         Appropriate energy
                         Team work
                         Does song lead from dialogue?

_____

                         Grade   Total

Further Remarks:

_____

_____

_____

_____

_____

Assignment 14

Complete the following student worksheet in preparation for performing the scene in Assignment 14. The emphasis in this assignment is on the words used by the character which create either humor or a certain sense of "style." It is the actor's facility with the language of the play which will greatly enhance the creation of the character. Interestingly the actor should notice that as vocal choices are made physical adjustments will occur. For instance, students using a Standard British dialect find their movements much more contained and executed in a higher altitude than when using a cockney dialect. Movement when using a cockney dialect tends to be looser, less controlled, and in a generally lower altitude.

With verbal humor, the element of repartée is crucial. To accomplish this, it is necessary for actors to be facile at picking up cues quickly. An exercise that is useful in accomplishing this goal is to have actors do a "pace" rehearsal. The cast is instructed to say their lines as quickly as possible and to begin each line on the last word of the preceding cue line. In other words, the actors are literally jumping on each other's lines. Practically speaking, the play would never be performed using such quick delivery but, if the cue pick up has been slow, the cast will get a clear idea of what is meant by the phrase "pick up your cues." This exercise is appropriate for any form of musical theatre in addition to High Musical Comedy.

Another useful exercise is to quickly throw a ball back and forth among the characters who are speaking to each other. You cannot speak until you have the ball in hand. This is a good exercise not only for cue pick up but for developing energy and assisting in a sense of ensemble. It's also a lot of fun!

Choose a High Musical Comedy from the following list or select one of your own. Select from it a scene five to ten minutes in length for three or more characters with dialogue which leads to a group song. Identify the verbal elements of humor in the dialogue. Compare and contrast the dialogue and lyrics of the characters, noting similarities and differences. Do these add to the humor? How? Do any of the characters use a specific dialect or colloquialisms or slang expressions? Does this add to the humor? How? What codes of social behavior and/or morals do the characters exemplify? Perform the scene with your partners.

Applause	*Kiss Me, Kate*	*Man with a Load of Mischief*
First Impressions	*Lady in the Dark*	*One Touch of Venus*

Suggestions by Instructor during scene preparation: _____

_____

_____

_____

Assignment 14
Student Worksheet

Name _____ Date _____

Character _____

Musical _____

Composers/Authors _____

Verbal element(s) of humor

    in dialogue:_____

    _____

    in lyrics:_____

    _____

Use of dialect, colloquialism, slang_____

_____

Dialogue similarities with other characters _____

_____

Differences from other characters _____

_____

Exemplified codes of behavior:

    a. Social _____

    _____

    b. Moral _____

Assignment 14
Sample Student Worksheet

Name _____ Date _____

Character _____ Molly _____

Musical _____ One Touch of Venus _____

Composers/Authors _Book by S.J. Perlman and Ogden Nash. Lyrics by Ogden Nash. Music by Kurt
Weill._____

Verbal element(s) of humor

    in dialogue: _____ employs hyperbole, quick wittedness, contemporary slang _____
_____

    in lyrics:___ classical references (Venus, Beatrice, Dante, DuBarry), wordplay (goddess, damsel,
cinch, pantie-pants), creates new word (odd-s)_____

Use of dialect, colloquialism, slang____ well-educated, Eastern dialect, urban _____
_____ "puss," "land sakes alive" (imitates non-urban slang), "blast"_____

Dialogue similarities with other characters __ She is most like Savory in her speech patterns. ___
_____

Differences from other characters ____ She is in strong contrast to Taxi, who is lower class Brooklyn.
She is given to the use of malapropisms._____

Exemplified codes of behavior:

    a.   Social __ Appearances are important. Self-control is a virtue. Emotion is dis-
guised._____

    b. Moral ___ There is more talk than action. The characters equate sexual patter with love. Venus
teaches them the meaning of romance._____

Assignment 14
Grading Sheet

Evaluation of Musical Acting Project _____

Students _____ Date _____

Title of Selection _____

Title of Song _____

Authors/Composers_____

Evaluation scale: 4 Excellent
                       3 Very Good
                       2 Good
                       1 Fair

Comments	**Specific Ratings**	**Score**
	Choice:	
	Dialogue and lyric:	
	a. Differentiation/similarity among characters	
	b. Dialect/slang	
	c. Projection of verbal humor	
	Appropriateness of gesture and movement	
	Clear projection of codes of behavior and/or morals	
	Team work	
	Sustaining energy through musical number	
	Grade Total	

Further Remarks:

_____

_____

_____

_____

Assignment 15

Choose a Contemporary Musical Comedy from the list in Assignment 12 or select one of your own. Select from it a scene, five to ten minutes in length, for two performers with dialogue which leads into a duet. (i.e. the scene between Will Parker and Ado Annie from *OKLAHOMA*! which leads into "With Me It's All or Nothin'.") Analyze the scene to determine which elements of all of the types of Musical Comedy are present.

In relation to Classical Musical Comedy the student should answer the following:
Are there character stereotypes from Classical Musical Comedy?
If there is humor in the scene, which comic device was employed?
Is it necessary to employ any elements of the actor's personality in developing the
character?

In relation to Musical Farce, the student should answer the following:
What are three adjectives to describe the physical movement of your character in the
scene?
What are three adjectives to describe your character's physical attitudes?

In relation to High Musical Comedy, the student should answer the following:
Are there any verbal elements of humor in the dialogue?
What are the exemplified social codes of behavior?
What are the exemplified moral codes of behavior?
Is there a use of dialect, colloquialism, or slang?

Once these questions have been addressed, prepare the scene and present it. The student's goal is to integrate all the elements found in the scene which derive from any of the types of Musical Comedy. Contemporary Musical Comedy puts together elements from all the forms of Musical Comedy and here is the student's opportunity to analyze how well it fits.

Instructor's comments:

_____

_____

_____

_____

Assignment 15
Grading Sheet

Evaluation of Musical Acting Project _____

Student Name _____

Character_____

Contemporary Musical Comedy Selection_____

Title of Song _____

Evaluation scale: 4 Excellent
                       3 Very Good
                       2 Good
                       1 Fair

Comments   **Specific Ratings**   **Score**

                    Integration of Muscal Comedy Elements:
                         Clear Stereotype, if present
                         Projection of humor, if any
                         Clear physicalization of character
                         Clear understanding of verbal humor
                         Clear projection of codes of
                              behavior and/or morals
                         Believability of Character
                         Team Work
                         Sustaining energy through
                              musical number
_____
                    Grade   Total

Further Remarks:

_____

_____

_____

_____

A. (Left) Notice the physicalization of humor evident in the characters on the right. They are surprised to see the Ghost, Tall Betsy.

B. (Right) Tall Betsy and the character, Dunce Baby, sustain energy through a musical number.

Figure 36. *TALL BETSY AND THE CRACKERBARREL TALES by Jacque Wheeler and Mariella Glenn Hartsfield. Directed by Jacque Wheeler for Valdosta State University. Published by Players Press.*

Figure 37. Photo from CABARET. Valdosta State University.

Chapter Seven

MEETING THE DEMANDS OF MUSICAL DRAMA

Unlike Musical Comedy, Musical Drama offers highly compressed plots, clearly established subplots, and complex, well developed characters. The songs and dances serve to further develop plot and/or character. Many Musical Dramas have comic elements in secondary characters and subplots, but these characters are well developed, and the subplots are carefully integrated into the musical as a whole. They do not divert the focus or interrupt the action as they may do in Musical Comedy.

The actor analyzes the dialogue and lyrics of a Musical Drama in much the same manner as he would a nonmusical drama. He must, however, always remember that the libretto is a highly compressed story and points are made more clearly and quickly than in nonmusical drama. The actor must first determine the goal, or super-objective, of the character. The **goal** is the one thing the actor defines as most important to the character (what the character wants above all else). Having determined the goal of his character, the actor then seeks to view each scene he appears in, in relation to this goal. He determines in each scene what action the character takes to achieve his goal, remembering that the action may occur in song or dance as well as dialogue. Each character may have forces which oppose or complicate the attainment of his goal. These forces may be human, environmental, social, supernatural, or self induced. An actor must ascertain which of these forces oppose his attainment of his goal. This opposition of forces constitutes conflict which is essential to the structure of Musical Drama.

Good Musical Dramas have conflicts which rise slowly in tension to the end of the first act and are resolved in the second act. The conflict is developed through a series of crises in which decisions are made or events occur which move the characters steadily toward the **climax** or moment of highest emotional intensity. In Musical Drama, the climax or crisis moment often takes place within a musical number. Since Musical Dramas, unlike Musical Comedies, have little or no extraneous material, a throughline of the action is easy to diagram. The character's throughline of action consists of the goals in each scene which lead to his super-objective, and the relation of those goals to the crises and climax of the Musical Drama.

One problem which an actor in Musical Drama encounters is the necessity of reestablishing a character. Since Musical Dramas are composed of relatively short scenes, audiences may have difficulty keeping track of characters who vanish from the action for a lengthy period. This problem quite often applies to secondary comic characters. The analysis of the character's throughline will help an actor overcome this problem. Another problem is that scenes of emotional intensity are presented with direct character-audience relationship, unlike their presentation in non-musical drama. In the latter, the audience merely observes the emotional scenes played intently by the performers. Musical Drama actors must remember not to exclude the audience while playing emotional scenes solely to each other. A 3/4 open body position is highly desirable in the presentation of the majority of these emotional scenes.

FIGURE 38. CAROUSEL, *original stars John Raitt and Jan Clayton. Even though the moment is intimate, the body positions are open to the audience.*

This open body position, however, should in no way hamper the actor's commitment to the emotional content of the scene he is playing or the song he is singing. In analyzing the emotional content of a song, it is important that the actor moves the character from one emotional level to another during the presentation of the lyric. If an actor determines a character is puzzled at the beginning of a song (as is the King in *THE KING AND I* singing "Puzzlement"), by the end of the song the character is either more puzzled, less puzzled, has resolved his puzzlement, or has moved to another emotion entirely. The character is not in the same emotional position he was in at the beginning of the song. It is this continued development of the rising and falling of emotional content that gives variety to the song and helps the actor to achieve a climactic moment in a song.

Another helpful technique in expressing the emotional content of a song or scene is for the actor to be aware of the opposition he encounters that inhibits his ability to achieve his goal in singing the song. To overcome this opposition, the actor employs different tactics and is either successful or fails with each one. At the end of the song or scene the audience should be aware of whether the character won or lost what he was seeking.

It is helpful for the actor to specify a relationship between the character and the audience [when singing a solo or delivering a monologue]. Does the character perceive the audience as "friend," "enemy," "co-conspirator," or "jury?" The possibilities are endless but a choice should be made.

The actor should also know what response the character desires from the audience. Does the character seek approval, disapproval, sympathy or applause from the audience? The more specific the actor can make his choices in these areas, the clearer will be the actor audience relationship.

It is in the area of Musical Drama that musical theatre most resembles non-musical theatre and where the technique employed by the actor is the closest to that employed by many actors in non-musical productions. The question of motivation is much more meaningful in Musical Drama than in the other areas of musical theatre because the libretto and score are very closely integrated and the structure of the text relies on cause and effect for its development.

While the characters in Musical Drama are often recognizably realistic, the framework of Musical Drama is nonrealistic. This framework includes sets, costumes, lighting, props, and the use of songs and dances. The actor must not allow these nonrealistic elements to distort his performance or the overall intent of the Musical Drama. One technique the actor may employ to maintain the realism of his character is to list his key speeches, songs and dances and to write out the thoughts that underlie the lines, lyrics and movements. The actor should write these thoughts in the first person, as if they were the thoughts of the character being portrayed.

In writing out the thoughts of the character, the actor should not comment on the character's state of mind. "She is frustrated because he is late." Rather, the actor writes in the present tense and not necessarily in complete sentences. "I wish he would come...Oh!...he is always late...he makes me so mad!...Oh! Here he comes. Mustn't show him I'm angry." These thoughts are written in a stream-of-consciousness style. These thoughts are termed the character's **subtext**. The actor should be aware that the character's thoughts occur when others are singing, speaking, or dancing as well. The primary source for any subtextual analysis begins in the text itelf and is then developed according to the actor's interpretation of the character. Consequently, no two actors would write exactly the same subtext for the same character.

Very often the motivation for an actor lies in the speech of another character immediately preceding a movement. An actor does not simply wait for his turn to speak. Just as in every day life we frequently talk to ourselves as others speak, in Musical Drama it is helpful to the actor to reflect on what the character is thinking while other characters speak. This helps the actor to develop the

Figure 39. Nicholas Wyman, Virginia Seidel, Charles Repole and Spring Fairbank (L to R) sing "Isn't It Great To Be Married" in VERY GOOD EDDIE. The Jerome Kern Musical Comedy courtesy of Goodspeed Opera House.

stimulus/response approach to acting. It also helps the actor to remember to **listen** when others are speaking. One of the greatest difficulties for an actor in musical or non-musical theatre is to remain in the specific moment of the play. Because we can read the script and know the next line or even the end, it is easy for actors to stop listening to each other once lines are memorized. It is the work of the actor to make each moment on stage appear as though it is happening for the first time. The following exercises will help the actor achieve this technique.

Figure 40.   A tender moment from BRIGADOON. *Robert Hays and Karen Flathers.*

Assignment 16

Choose a character from Musical Drama and construct the character's throughline of action. Identify the character's superobjective. Specifically note the crises and climax of the Musical Drama. Note specifically where props or costumes affect the achievement of the character's objectives. Possible Musical Drama characters are listed below. Others may be substituted if desired.

Female	Musicals	Male
Fiona	*Brigadoon*	Tommy, Harry
Sally Bowles, Fraulein Schneider	*Cabaret*	Cliff, Herr Schultz
Julie Jordan, Carrie Pipperidge	*Carousel*	Billy Bigelow, Mr. Snow
Anna, Tuptim, Lady Thiang	*King and I*	King
Louisa	*Fantasticks*	Matt
Golde, Yente, Hodel	*Fiddler on the Roof*	Tevye, Pirchek

NOTE: Some definitions helpful in the completion of this assignment include:

Crisis: A complication. A moment of discovery for a character where a choice of action must be made. There may be many crisis moments in a libretto. For principal characters there are more crisis moments than for secondary characters and the Musical Drama includes the crises of all characters.

Climax: Moment of highest emotional intensity. This moment may vary from production to production and depends on the director's point of view. Also, principal characters may have a climactic moment of their own which may or may not be the same as the climactic moment in the text.

Attainment: Achieving one's superobjective. Not all characters achieve their superobjective. There is a moment, usually near the end of the production, when the character realizes whether they have either won or lost their superobjective.

Assignment 16 (Sample)
Nellie Forbush

The following is a sample scene by scene breakdown of the throughline of action for the character of Nellie Forbush in *SOUTH PACIFIC*.

Superobjective: To find the right man to love.

Throughline of action:

Act I, i:	Nellie admits her attraction to the older, more sophisticated French man, Emile de Becque.
Act I, iii:	Nellie establishes her naive, uncomplicated, and trusting personality through her interaction with fellow nurses and seabees.
Act I, v:	Nellie discusses Emile with Capt. Bracket. She comes to the realization that she knows little about Emile.
Act I, vi:	Nellie considers the differences between her past and Emile's past.
Act I, vii:	(First Crisis)
	Nellie decides to "wash that man right out of her hair," but when he proposes she confesses to being "in love with a wonderful guy."
Act I, viii:	Nellie confesses her love to the nurses.
Act I, xiii:	(Second Crisis)
	Nellie discovers that Emile has half-caste children and breaks off the relationship.
Act II, i:	Nellie focuses her energies on the Thanksgiving show to forget Emile.
Act II, iii:	Nellie performs in the Thanksgiving show for the same reason.
Act II, iv:	(Climax)
	Nellie tells Emile that she cannot overcome the differences between them.
Act II, viii:	(Third Crisis)
	Nellie discovers that Emile is in danger and realizes she still loves him.
Act II, ix:	Nellie fears Emile may be dead.
Act II, x:	Nellie tells Mary and Liat that Joe is dead. Her own fears for Emile become intensified.
Act II, xii:	(Attainment)
	Nellie and Emile are reunited.

Note that Nellie's actions scene by scene are related to her super-objective. In relation to costuming and props, Nellie's military costuming does not mitigate her youth and femininity. Her evening dress for Emile's party establishes Nellie's possible role as a wife and a hostess. Her oversized sailor outfit for the Thanksgiving entertainment emphasizes the difference between the masculine world in which Nellie finds herself and the small hometown and mother she left in Little Rock, Arkansas. The use of the shampoo prop allows for a physicalization of Nellie's decision to end the relationship with Emile.

Assignment 17

Choose a monologue and song from a Musical Drama and write the subtext. These underlying thoughts should be written in the first person as if the character were speaking about himself and his responses to persons, places, and events around him. Note the relationship of the monologue and song to the character's objective in the scene and to the super-objective. Note the relationship of the monologue and song to the musical's crises and climax. The following is a list of suggested characters, but others may be substituted if desired.

Female	Musicals	Male
Elizabeth Barrett	*Robert and Elizabeth*	Robert Browning
Guinevere	*Camelot*	Arthur, Lancelot
Aldonza	*Man of La Mancha*	Don Quixote, Sancho
Rose, Louise	*Gypsy*	Herbie
Nellie	*South Pacific*	Emile, Lt. Cable
Baby Love, Dolly	*The Grass Harp*	Colin
Mabel Normand	*Mack and Mabel*	Mack Sennett

It will be helpful for the actor to identify the relationship between the character and the audience as outlined in the chapter. A desired response from the audience should be chosen and the character either *wins* the desired response or *loses* the desired response.

In choosing objectives, keep the stakes as high as possible. The more important an objective is for the actor the more important the character becomes to the audience. Verbs like *to convince*, *to annihilate* or *to celebrate* are strong verbs that suggest strong action choices.

To aid in this winning or losing, it is important for the actor to be affected by the monologue. No character is precisely the same at the end of a monologue as he/she was before the monologue. It is just this progression of the character through the monologue that moves, not only the character forward, but the action of the play as well. To assist in this progression the monologue should be analyzed in terms of where the character makes new discoveries during the speech. The more discoveries made by the character in the present moment (that is, as the character speaks before the audience), the more immediate the monologue becomes for the audience.

Assignment 17 (Sample)

Character: Rose

Musical: *Gypsy*

Monologue and Song: End of Act One monologue leading into "Everything's Coming Up Roses," the finale to Act I

Rose's super-objective is to celebrate her children as stars — to convince other people to notice them. Initially she focuses her energies on her daughter, June. When June leaves, immediately preceding the above mentioned monologue, she then focuses her energy on her other daughter, Louise.

The subtext for the monologue continuing into the song would greatly differ according to the actress playing the role. One approach would include the following thoughts. The underlying emotional content of the song is dual. On one hand Rose attempts to convince Louise that Louise can be a star and on the other hand, Rose completes her own re-direction of energy, rejecting and dismissing June and aligning herself with Louise.

Sample subtext monologue: "June...how could she leave? After all I've done for her? Sacrificed... Given up...ungrateful, stupid, foolish girl... Oh my baby — June. What will I do without you? No. I won't cry. I've cried enough in my life...etc."

NB: The speech and song are also appropriate for Assignment 18 as they occur at the crisis moment at the end of Act One.

Figure 41. GYPSY, Glassboro Summer Theatre. Author Jacque Wheeler is center.

Assignment 18

Choose a speech leading into a song which occurs at crisis, climax, or attainment of super-objective point in a Musical drama. Perform the sequence for evaluation.

One example would be Dolly's farewell to Ephraim, leading into "Before the Parade Passes By," the finale to Act One in *Hello, Dolly!* Dolly firmly commits herself to living in the present and future, releasing herself from the past.

Assignment 18
Grading Sheet

Evaluation of Musical Acting Project _____

Student _____ Date _____

Musical Drama _____

Author/Composer _____

Evaluation Scale: 4 Excellent
                      3 Very Good
                      2 Good
                      1 Fair

Comments	**Specific Ratings**	**Score**
	Choice	
	Communication of subtext	
	Communication of character	
	Communication of mood and tone	
	Projection of appropriate emotional intensity	
	Singing technique	
	Sustaining of character through song	
	Grade Total	

Further Remarks:

_____

_____

_____

Assignment 19

Choose a scene from a Musical Drama centering on emotion. The selection should be five to ten minutes long and feature two or more characters. The selection must include a group song, although a musical scene (see Chapter 1) may be substituted. The presentation of the scene should indicate that the performers have analyzed carefully and have shared their insights with each other during rehearsals.

**Assignment 19
Grading Sheet**

Evaluation of Musical Acting Project _____

Students _____ Date _____

Title of Musical Drama _____ Title of Song _____

Author/Composer _____

Central Emotion of Scene _____

Objectives in Scene _____

Evaluation Scale: 4   Excellent
                   3   Very Good
                   2   Good
                   1   Fair

Comments	Specific Rating	Score
	Choice	
	Communication of emotions	
	Projection of characters:	
	a. clear subtexts	
	b. clear objectives	
	c. appropriate emotional intensity	
	d. sustaining of characters through song	
	Vocal technique	
	Communication of mood & tone	
	Team work	
	Grade Total	

Further Remarks:

_____

_____

_____

Figure 42. THE STUDENT PRINCE. *The happy life is not long for Karl Franz, heir to the throne. His student days' barmaid, Kathie, is played by Leigh Munro, while Jack Tussel presents the Prince. Courtesy of the Los Angeles Music Center.*

Chapter Eight

THE MAGIC KINGDOMS: OPERETTA

The recognizably realistic musical dramas are nowhere to be found among the stereotypes who dwell in the mythical kingdoms of the operetta. These are the lands of princes and princesses, dukes and duchesses, comic prime ministers, and meddling servants, many or all of them invariably disguised. Merry widows cavort in exotic locales, and comic con men and swaggering soldiers pursue diminutive damsels through greensward and glades.   How then is the musical actor to play such whimsical and fantastic creatures?

For many years, this was not a problem. The operetta had declined in popularity until the Broadway revival of *The Pirates of Penzance* in the late 1970's. The works of Gilbert and Sullivan, which even high schools had dropped in favor of the latest Broadway musical, became fashionable again. Moreover, as professional producers realized, not only were operettas tuneful and glamorous, most of them were now royalty free, having passed sufficient birthdays to become public domain. Consequently, the past half dozen years has seen the return of the operetta form in the classic sense of *The Desert Song*, *The Student Prince*, the Gilbert and Sullivan repertoire, and of such later incarnations as *Kismet* and *The Song of Norway*.

The musical actor must remember that the magic kingdoms of operetta are romantic and lyrical. They contain a labyrinth of complex musical numbers (quartets, sextets, etc.) and only the strongest singers can have passports to these enchanted and enchanting locales. Analysis of the libretto of the operetta is not easy, for since the operetta contains far more music than dialogue, the personalities of the characters are created more by what and how they sing than by what they say and do. Look, then, for clues to character behavior and clear presentation of character

Figure 43. H. M. S. PINAFORE. *North Carolina School of the Arts. Photo by C. Buchanan.*

to the audience in the musical scenes. Operettas contain many more musical scenes — those sequences which combine music, pantomime, dialogue, and dance or stylized movement - than the other forms of musical theatre. These musical scenes often compress emotion into high levels of intensity with little apparent psychological motivation. There is, in fact, little of the logically developed conflict of the musical drama, even though the operetta plot may be essentially serious; rather, the development of conflict in the operetta is not determined by cause and effect. These characters do not develop as the characters do in musical drama, but more closely resemble the character types in musical comedy, though they have been elevated to higher social status and the foreign settings place them at a further distance from reality. This social status and foreign setting elevate the characters to a more unique position than musical comedy characters, making them potentially more interesting for the truly creative musical theatre actor to portray.

The following checklist will prove beneficial as you read the operetta and attempt to discern what clues are available for the portrayal of the character.

I.   To what extent is the author intending to project reality? What kind of events interest the author, commonplace or strange? What principles of everyday behavior are evident in these far-fetched plots and exotic characters? Can oddities of character, behavior, or perspective of life be better explained by the context of the exotic setting? How can the actor integrate his personal point of view of reality with the author's perception of reality?

II.   Does the operetta exist solely for the purpose of entertainment, as most of them do, or does it reveal a new experience or assess an old one? What are the systems of values and moral codes which the operetta suggests? How does it suggest them? Are they exemplified by certain characters? What can the musical actor do to project or elaborate upon them? Do their values make them sympathetic or unsympathetic to each other? To the audience?

III. Since operetta characters usually represent universally recognizable types, how can they be made vocally or physically unique? What is the character type? Do their names, titles, or occupations suggest their personalities? How can the emotions and values expressed by what they sing be projected physically through movement and gesture? How does the character relate specifically to the advancement of the plot?

IV. Can the actor find similarities between the setting of the operetta and locations which he has personally experienced? What change in normal behavior is observable in these new surroundings? In dress code? In etiquette? If they have no relation to anything recognizable, how can the recognizable be adapted, amplified, and heightened?

Just as in any other musical theatre form, it is necessary to analyze the layout of the score.

In addition, the following questions need to be answered about the score of the operetta.

I. What are the complexities of the songs (i.e. duet, trio, recitative) that cause them to differ from more modern musical theatre types?

II. What portion of the score is potentially the most difficult for the individual actor to sing? Why? How can the actor sustain the emotion through lengthy musical phrases, both sung and unsung?

III. What portions of the score require expanded breath control because of lengthier musical phrases?

Though the characters are not as close to real life as the characters in Musical Drama, the actor can still employ some of the techniques used in Musical Drama. The actor can determine a goal for the character for each song he/she sings. The songs become more meaningful for both actor and audience if they are done with purpose. A song might be to convince, to celebrate, or to tell a story, or any one of dozens of strong verb choices. The actor can, also, still determine his relationship with the audience in solo work. Are they friend or foe or confidante?

Since the characters **do** resemble characters in Musical Comedy, the actor can employ techniques suggested earlier in Chapter Six. Reviewing the lists of Physical Attitudes and Movement terms from Chapter Two is also helpful. Specific choices should be made by the actor in terms of the attitude of the character and movement patterns. Characterizations will be more fully dimensional if the actor makes more than one attitudinal choice for the character.

In attempting to sustain emotion through a long musical phrase, the actor may find it helpful to articulate the subtext of the piece. The subtext may assist the actor in understanding the emotional content of the song and also give him something to focus on in addition to holding a note for twelve counts or waiting four measures before his next vocal entrance. The music in operettas is more exciting if there is a forward progression to it — that is, the audience feels like the music is taking them somewhere. They learn more about the plot or character or the song reveals something about the atmosphere of the play. The most important point for the actor is that no character is unaffected by any song he or she sings. The character should be somehow changed by the song. If the character is in love at the beginning of the song he or she is either more in love or less in love by the end. If a character is angry at the beginning of a song, he or she either becomes more angry or less angry by the end of the song. **No** character is exactly the same at the end of a song as he or she was at the beginning of a song.

Musical theatre actors often have the embarrassing feeling that they are overacting when preparing to perform operetta characters. They need to remember that operettas are similar in style to the Restoration comedies and melodrama of the non-musical theatre. The grandeur of the settings and emotions, the elaborateness of the costumes and props, and the lushness and abundance of the music demand a heightened performance style characterized by largeness of gestures and clearly discernible choices, unfettered by realistic subtleties, on the part of the actor. The magic kingdoms of operetta are for the adventurous, not the timid, performer.

Figure 44. Photo from Valdosta State University's production of PIRATES OF PENZANCE .

Assignment 20

Choose a portion of a well-known fairy tale which utilizes three characters. Identify the stereotype for each character using one noun and one adjective per type. (Example: henpecked husband, meddling servant, young lover, etc.). Pantomime the sequence, placing special emphasis on the extraordinary elements presented by the locale and status of the characters. Repeat the sequence two more times, rotating characters each time. (It may be necessary during the rotation for a male to portray female and vice versa.)

For example, in *Rapunzel*, the characters would be identified in the following manner: Rapunzel, the "innocent maiden," threatened by the "wicked witch," is saved by the Prince, her "young lover."

Assignment 20
Grading Sheet

Evaluation of Musical Acting Project _____

Students _____ Date _____

Evaluation Scale: 4 Excellent
                       3 Very Good
                       2 Good
                       1 Fair

Comments	**Specific Ratings**	**Score**
	Verbal Identification of Stereotypes	
	Physicalization of stereotype:	
	a. movement	
	b. gesture	
	c. posture	
	Clear distinction among the three	
	stereotypes presented:	
	Ensemble work	
	Clarity of story sequence	

Grade   Total

Further Remarks:

_____

_____

_____

Assignment 21

Using the original character type selected for assignment 20, choose two solo songs from two operettas which are performed by the same character type. If possible, try to choose contrasting selections; one comic, one serious. On a separate sheet answer the questions pertaining to musical score from this chapter. Present the songs adhering in character type to movement and gesture. For example, for the male "young lover": the serious song, Danillo's "The Merry Widow Waltz" from *The Merry Widow* would contrast the comic song "Colorado Love Call" sung by Captain Jim in *Little Mary Sunshine*. For example, in the role of an ambitious meddler, Ruth sings in *Pirates of Penzance* in a comic vein and Lalume in *Kismet* sings "Rahadlakum" in a more serious vein.

Assignment 21
Grading Sheet

Evaluation of Musical Acting Project _____

Student _____ Date _____

Title of Operettas _____

Title of Songs _____

Authors/Composers _____

Evaluation Scale: 4 Excellent
                       3 Very Good
                       2 Good
                       1 Fair

Comments	**Specific Ratings**	**Score**
	Choices	
	Clarity of stereotypes	
	Written analysis of score	
	Clear distinction between selections	
	Physicalization of stereotype:	
	a. movement	
	b. gesture	
	c. posture	
	Vocal technique (pitch, etc.)	
	Breath control	

Grade   Total

Further Remarks:

_____

_____

Figure 45.   A design for a make-up character similar to that used in Andrew Lloyd Webber's CATS.   NOTE: The hair is teased to shape and the face is a make-up, not a prosthetic piece. Make-up by Joe Rossi & Company courtesy of Mehron, Inc. Photo from "Players Press: Stage Make-Up Techniques."

Chapter Nine

THE LATEST ARRIVAL:
BROADWAY OPERA

There is no validity to those critics who say that there is nothing new on the musical theatre scene. Indeed, the musical theatre's most recent blessed event has not even come of age yet, though its contemporary roots were planted by *Porgy and Bess* over fifty years ago. Not until the mid 1970's did the new genre successfully blossom for musical theatre audiences into what is now termed Broadway Opera. Like the operetta, the Broadway Opera emphasizes difficult music, but unlike the operetta, the music stems from popular and recognizable sources: the Latin rhythms of *Evita*, the classic rock rhythms of *Jesus Christ Superstar*, and the hybrid rock and country and western rhythms of *Joseph and the Amazing Technicolor Dreamcoat*. While the operetta is glamorous by nature of locality and situation, the Broadway Opera is spectacular in style and treatment. While *The Merry Widow* has one act entirely set in the garden of a Parisian embassy, for example, Evita shows us the same incident, a political speech, in triplicate from the points of view of the political figures, the assembled crowd, and the narrator, by the juxtaposition of revolving set pieces, film loops, and projections. While the operetta may include dance (how can *The Merry Widow* exist without her waltz?), dance in the Broadway Opera is part of the continual flow of movement, both of character and scenery, which sets this genre of musical theatre apart from its fellows. While *Porgy and Bess* has its musical roots in the blues and spirituals of African Americans and thus qualifies as the first of the Broadway Operas, its successors have veered away from realism of character and scenery into the non-realism characteristic of the German Theatre of the 1920s. The production style of Broadway Opera is experimental and flamboyant. Gone is the romantic tone of the operetta, replaced by a sometimes serious, sometimes whimsical viewpoint of human existence.

Composer Andrew Lloyd Webber popularized this new form of musical theatre, even to the extent of having three Broadway operas (*Evita*, *Cats*, and *Joseph and the Amazing Technicolor Dreamcoat*) running concurrently on Broadway during the 1980s. The additional success of Stephen Sondheim's *Sweeney Todd* proved that this type of musical theatre is here to stay. Sondheim has also added the element of intellectual stimulation to the Broadway Opera. He is credited with developing the **Concept Musical** where all elements of plot, character, dance, and spectacle are organized around an idea. It is this "idea" which contributes to the integration of the libretto and the score. In *Sunday In The Park With George*, the concept centers around "art" — what it is, how it is produced and how artistic concepts change. *Into The Woods* combines several well-known fairy tales, intricately weaving them together, adding new characters and forming an original tale celebrating the theme that life is a struggle but we are not alone. In Sondheim's early work, *A Little Night Music*, he unifies the score by composing all the music in 3/4 time. Since the Broadway Opera allows for this element of experimentation, the musical theatre actor, then, is faced with problems that will continue to change as more Broadway Operas are produced.

The world of the most recent Broadway Operas is the world of imagination (symbols, metaphors, dreams, fantasies), and various aspects of the visual arts (colors, shapes, textures, lines, multimedia devices). While Broadway Opera is closely linked to the society for which it is produced and attempts to mirror and reflect the attitudes, philosophies, and basic assumptions of its audience, its frequent use of metaphors and symbols keeps the audience at a distance, making the appeal more to the intellect than to the emotions. The Broadway opera actor, then, must bridge the emotional distance to the audience and avoid being dwarfed by the sometimes overpowering technical elements of the production. He must remember that even though the character may be historical (Eva Peron, Judas) or literary (Rum Tum Tugger) in precedent, the truth of the character exists solely in the perception of the audience. The character, then, must relate to current values and beliefs, and the actor must understand the character in relation to the culture for which it exists, as well as the culture from which it came. Because this Broadway Opera is so new and constantly changing, the interpretation of the characters is, likewise, more fluid and open to change than the characters of other musical theatre forms.

In order to project these characters, the actor needs to develop a strong sense of body awareness and physical dexterity. His actions need to be concise, clear-cut and large enough to overcome the spectacular production style. In addition, the actor may have to examine the score in order to ascertain what vocal restrictions may result from the physical demands of the production. Prerecording may be necessary in the more elaborate Broadway Operas when the demands of the score and the physical production conflict. It would be foolhardy for a musical theatre performer to refuse to recognize that he cannot achieve vocal techniques that could not be achieved in the original production. The problem for the actor lies in determining where he must conserve energy (through prerecording, amplification, doubling of voices), and where he must enlarge energy to project the character in spite of the production's distractions. The actor will find it helpful to make a diagram of the script and score noting scenes and songs that present potential problems. The vocal problems need to be discussed with the musical director; the physical problems need to be discussed with the director. In outlining his character's objectives and subtexts, the actor needs to relate those specifically to current events, attitudes, or fads

Figure 46. JOSEPH AND THE AMAZING TECHNICOLOR DREAMCOAT *Jekyll Island Musical Theatre Festival.*

which may affect the audience relationship with the character. For example, the narrator of *Joseph and the Amazing Technicolor Dreamcoat* is not specified clearly. Therefore, it might be a television evangelist, a close captioned television anchor, or a bag person, and all of these of either sex or of any age. The qualities which Eva Peron exhibits are less the qualities of the real woman than those to which an audience will respond affirmatively or negatively depending on their reactions to recent publicity concerning dictatorships or foreign political figures: Gorbachev's world peace plan, Arab terrorism, for example. To the nonhuman characters of some Broadway Operas (cats, trains) the musical theatre actor must project those same physicalizations which match qualities in their human counterparts—strength, lust, glamour—just as he would embody the virtues or vices of miracle or morality plays. At the moment, the characterizing of Broadway operas is a stimulating challenge and will continue to be so until the category becomes as stable as the other types of musicals, if, indeed, it ever does. For in the past, musical theatre experiences were relatively uniform for an equally uniform society. But in contemporary musical theatre, they are as varied in content and purpose as the audience.

Figure 47. NUNSENSE. Jekyll Island Musical Theatre Festival

Assignment 22

As a preparation for the possibility of prerecording, obtain a recording of a political speech. Your library may have recordings from John F. Kennedy, Franklin D. Roosevelt, Martin Luther King, or Adolph Hitler, or you may simply record a political speech from a current political figure. Then: (1) memorize the speech and lip sync the delivery, adding posture and gestures to reinforce the underlying emotional content as well as the message of the speech; and (2) pantomime an audience member listening to and reacting to the delivery of the speech. Conclude the pantomime by making clear either agreement or disagreement with the message of the speech and the personality of the speaker. N.B. An interesting extension of this assignment would be to have several students pantomime audience reaction to the same speech and interact as a group.

In completing this assignment, the actor will need to employ his powers of observation. It is extremely helpful to watch a videotape of the speech, if it is available, or to make your own if the choice involves a current political figure. As you view the videotape, make notes on the following points:

1.   Head position: (nodding, leaning to one side, chin lowered, etc.)

_____

_____

2.   Use of hands: Identify the quality of gesture with a verb. (pointing, stabbing, circling, etc.) _____

_____

3.   Relationship of speaker to podium or table. (Leaning, standing to one side, etc.)

_____

_____

4.   Speaker's responses to audience. (Is speaker trying to convince audience? Does audience arouse emotion in speaker such as anger, frustration, or pleasure?) _____

_____

_____

5.   If discernible, what is the audience's response to the speaker? _____

_____

_____

Assignment 22
Grading Sheet

Evaluation of Musical Acting Project _____

Student _____ Date _____

Speaker _____

Evaluation Scale: 4 Excellent
                     3 Very Good
                     2 Good
                     1 Fair

Comments	**Specific Ratings**	**Score**
	Choice	
	Physicalization of speech's message	
	Physicalization of emotion of speaker	
	Appropriate characterization of speaker	
	Appropriate characterization of audience member	
	Clear projection of audience members' attitude at the conclusion of the speech	

                              Grade   Total

Further Remarks:

_____

_____

_____

_____

_____

Assignment 23

Choose a song from a Broadway Opera. Choose appropriate movement to suggest the character and the intent of the song. Add the element of distraction to your performance and sustain the vocalization and the physicalization while a group of classmates plays musical chairs, the Farmer in the Dell, or London Bridge quietly around the singer. At completion of the exercise, discuss the problems presented, including those things experienced by the performer and those things experienced by the group members.

Student Worksheet

Name _____ Date _____

Character _____

Broadway Opera _____

Analysis of Character _____

_____

_____

Classification of song _____

3 adjectives describing physical attitudes

_____

_____

_____

3 adjectives describing movement

_____

_____

_____

Assignment 24

Choose a song, not necessarily from Broadway Opera or even Musical Theatre, which has a recognizable musical tradition (i.e. a spiritual, a country western song, a rock and roll song, etc.). Perform the song suggesting qualities representing any object from the following list:

rag doll	washing machine
bear	puppy
wind up toy	fire engine
bird	police car
weather vane	elephant
tiger	ball

Be specific in your physical choices to suggest particulars about your object. What kind of ball? What breed of puppy? What is the age of the washing machine? Likewise be specific in vocal choices. What kinds of sounds might these items emit? Use any appropriate qualities in the interpretation of the song. The vocal and physical embodiment should be appropriate to the musical tradition.

This assignment will be particularly helpful to actors who are inhibited and need to work on the technique of relaxation. The objects above, being non-human, allow for a great extension of the imagination, and, hopefully, a physical and vocal release because there is less concern for what is realistic. While the choices need to be specific, they can also be outrageous. In the land of such fantasy, anything is possible. The problem is to embody the qualities of the objects — the limpness and blank expression of a Rag Doll, perhaps with a broken heart, singing "My Funny Valentine" using very loose, disconnected movement, or the creaky, turning, cranking quality of an old 1920's washing machine on a back porch in Texas singing "Achy Breaky Heart." Instructors may choose to do this as an improvisation for the class. A single song may be selected and different class members may choose different objects to interpret the song.

Instructor comments or suggestions:

_____

_____

_____

_____

_____

_____

Assignment 24
Grading Sheet

Evaluation of Musical Acting Project _____

Student _____ Date _____

Title of Song _____

Choice of Object _____

Evaluation Scale: 4 Excellent
                   3 Very Good
                   2 Good
                   1 Fair

Comments   **Specific Ratings**   **Score**

                          Choice of song
                          Choice of object
                          Physicalization of the object
                          Vocalization of the object
                          Vocal technique
                          Breath control
                          Sustaining of energy
                          Creativity in choice and
                                execution of the assignment

                          Grade   Total

Further Remarks:

_____

_____

_____

_____

_____

_____

_____

Figure 48. Christina Avila and Grant Goodeve (pre- EIGHT IS ENOUGH), *performing the "Amsterdam" song from* JACQUES BREL IS ALIVE AND WELL AND LIVING IN PARIS, *produced by William-Alan Landes. Photo courtesy of Players U.S.A.*

Chapter Ten

HIGHLIGHTING THE HYBRIDS:
THE REVUE, THE SYMPHONIC DRAMA AND THE PLAY WITH MUSIC

If the Broadway Opera is the most recent and the most in transition of the purer musical theatre genres, then the revue is the oldest of the American musical theatre contributions, tracing its roots to the minstrel show dating from the 1840s. While Vaudeville and burlesque also developed from the minstrel show, the revue remains the longest lasting of these earlier forms. The revue's loose format, which blends songs, dances, and sketches tied together by theme, has always been popular with audiences, whether in the elaborate tradition of Florenz Ziegfeld or the more intimate tradition of *The Garrick Gaieties*. The latter type made an easy transition to Off-Broadway, and later proved especially popular on television. Television, however, sounded the death knell of the revue in its original form, and while the form is retained to some extent on cruise ships and in cabarets, the more popular revues in recent years have altered the format. Some, such as *Pump Boys and Dinettes*, blend similar types of music, others such as *Ain't Misbehavin'*, *Berlin to Broadway*, and *Side by Side by Sondheim* contain only the works of one composer tied together by narration Thus, the new form of revue places its predominant emphasis on music, and characterization, no longer developed in sketches, must now be established by the wider range of songs required of the performer. While the performer in a classical revue might only do a half dozen songs, and those of an extremely similar nature, the current revue performer may well sing four times as many songs of widely contrasting types and also narrate the transitions between numbers. Thus the contemporary revue requires a great deal of musical versatility on the part of the actor, as well as shifting the focus of characterization from the now eliminated sketches to the songs themselves. Thus the balance of score and libretto which once made the revue close to musical comedy has changed dramatically in recent years, creating a hybrid musical type which is closer to the radio shows of the 1930s, although in a more visual form.

Unlike its hybrid counterpart, the symphonic drama is relatively new in the history of musical theatre. This form was created and titled in the late 1930s by Paul Green, who for many years dominated the symphonic drama as Andrew Lloyd Webber has recently dominated the Broadway opera. The symphonic drama is limited solely to outdoor performance, and, for many years, was primarily limited to the Southeast in location. This unique blending of American history with period song and dance is elaborate in sets and costumes and entails a large cast of performers often numbering above fifty. Spectacular battle scenes and elaborate stage effects abound, and even if the role is small, the personage played is usually famous enough to be immediately recognized by the large number of tourists who flock to these summer productions. The symphonic dramas offer summer employment to thousands of young musical theatre performers who have used them as stepping stones to careers in the legitimate theatre. In recent years as this hybrid has expanded to the southwest, the productions now serve as showcases for film and television careers as well.

Symphonic drama performers find themselves playing distillations of famous historical figures rather than well rounded characters. Their roles never differ from the public's preconceptions of the characters, preconceptions which often are founded on legend rather than fact. Quite often the actor complains that the symphonic drama characters are one dimensional, and that the musical selections are extremely limited in type and repetitive in musical structure. Large choral numbers frequently occur and individual characters are generally assigned only one type of musical number. The musical numbers serve primarily to create and enhance the historical atmosphere of the productions. For this reason the music for symphonic drama is usually music from the actual period rather than original music composed for the production. The music also serves to underline the emotions of the characters, and since these emotions are not widely varied, the actor often feels that his role is restricted by the music rather than expanded by it. However, there is much to be learned from appearing in symphonic drama: the handling of period props and costumes, the mastering of the projection of a character in a large amphitheatre to an audience of thousands and the opportunity to experience the sustaining of a character over a run of several

Figure 49.   Servant scene in tavern, SHE STOOPS TO CONQUER, *Valdosta State University.*

months, rare for the fledgling musical theatre actor. All of these combine to give invaluable training. The musical theatre performer may complain that research for the symphonic drama character is shallow and limited to externals, but it also gives a groundwork in historical research that is often necessary in other forms of musical theatre.

The tradition of the play with music is even older than its fellow hybrids. It has been a part of theatre history since the days of Shakespeare. The emphasis is primarily on the text, and incidental music is supplied by characters who logically would sing (jesters, court musicians, tavern entertainers) or central characters when song can enhance the emotional atmosphere of a particular scene (Ophelia's "mad song," Desdemona's "willow song"). In the more contemporary plays with music, such as those of Bertolt Brecht, the few songs are used to serve as commentary on the action or transition between the episodes. The fact is that in both symphonic dramas and plays with music the musical numbers might sometimes be deleted without seriously damaging the production as a whole.

Musical theatre actors often fail to take advantage of the opportunities offered by the latter two musical theatre hybrids. Both offer training in projection of and sustaining of character while at the same time allowing musical experiences which are less intense and less demanding than in a full scale musical. These productions are ideally suited for beginning musical theatre actors who need to develop their musical skills.

Appearing in a revue is another ideal opportunity for a beginning musical theatre actor. The revue enables the actor to gauge his ability to establish rapport with an audience and to identify his public personality, both of which will prove extremely helpful as he progresses into the more complicated musical theatre forms.

However helpful these hybrids might be to the fledgling actor, they pose problems as well; albeit problems which, when solved, enable the musical theatre actor to approach more complicated forms with a greater sense of assurance. Musical revues, for example, require almost chameleon like changes from song to song, while the narration demands charm and energy in order to avoid becoming merely dull exposition. Since revue casts are almost always small in number, the ability to sustain energy, while remaining on stage for extended periods of time, is crucial. In addition, as the production elements of costume and scenery are minimal, if indeed they are present at all, the burden of character change rests completely on the actor's own physical resources, thus placing equally great demands on his tools of observation and imagination.

In symphonic drama, conversely, with its emphasis on elaborate sets and costumes of bygone eras, with its enormous cast of performers, and with its large audience so far removed from the playing area, the actor faces the opposite problem. He must bridge the great distance from the audience, he must not be overwhelmed by the spectacle of the production, and he must not be lost in the throngs of other performers when he should be the center of focus.

In the play with music the actor's performance includes justifying musical selections that may not be well integrated in the text. Consequently, he must make the music seem logical to its situation and environment, and not merely an unnecessary distraction.

Figure 50. NUNSENSE, Jekyll Island Musical Theatre Festival, directed by Jacque Wheeler.

Assignment 25

Choose a song from any musical by Rodgers and Hammerstein, Cole Porter, Stephen Sondheim, Frank Lesser or Jerry Herman. Prepare the song using two different dramatic persona. Observe people in a restaurant or on the street. Choose two persons who might logically sing your song. Write a brief paragraph describing the person as accurately as possible and hypothesize a situation in which they might sing the song. Write a paragraph analyzing your own personality as well, emphasizing any aspects which you think are particularly appropriate in interpreting the song. Present the song in both situations. Then present the song using only your own personality. (For example, using the song "Shall We Dance?" the following dramatic persons and situations might be employed: child in dance class, teenager at a sock hop, man or wife at fiftieth wedding anniversary, young single person at a disco.)

As you write your observation take special care to note the quality of gestures or movement. Do not say "she moved her hands a lot when she spoke." It is more helpful to note that "when she spoke her hands moved in a circular fashion, making graceful, bird-like swoops through the air" or "she stabbed at her food with her fork making loud clanging noises on her plate." Be as specific and descriptive as you can. Be sure to note posture and the attitude suggested by the posture you observe. If you have trouble putting your observations into words, use the lists in Chapter Two to help you.

Many actors find the use of imagery helpful in their observation. "He moved like a big bear; she moved like a graceful swan; his actions were jagged and jerky and reminded me of the color red." These images are sometimes very helpful in the creation of the physicalization of the character. Actors like to use animal imagery. Several improvisational situations are appropriate in developing these images for practical use. First imagine yourself as the animal you associate with the character. Move about as the animal in its natural habitat. Next make notations of three qualities describing the way the animal moved. (For example if the character is reminiscent of a "Bear," three things you might discover as you move like the bear are: 1) Bears are heavy-footed. 2) Bears move slowly. 3) Bears "paw" at the air when angry. The discoveries will be as varied as the specific animal you become.) Next move about the space as you normally would. Finally, add the three qualities you noted regarding the animal to your movement. In the case of the Bear, your movement would become slower and heavier, and your gestures would have a "pawing" quality, perhaps lashing out in the air. The movement of the character will be decidedly different than your own.

Instructor comments or suggestions:

_____

_____

_____

_____

_____

_____

Assignment 25
Grading Sheet

Evaluation of Musical Acting Project _____

Student _____ Date _____

Title of Song _____

Composer _____

Evaluation Scale: 4 Excellent
                        3 Very Good
                        2 Good
                        1 Fair

Comments	**Specific Ratings**	**Score**
	Choice	
	Descriptive paragraphs	
	Physical embodiment of characters	
	Clear character differentiation	
	Appropriate use of actor's personality	
	Focus of energy	
	Vocal technique	
	Grade	Total

Further Remarks:

_____

_____

_____

_____

_____

Assignment 26

Choose an historical figure from the following list. Select a song from the appropriate historical period. (Do not use songs from the musical theatre repertoire.) Prepare the song attempting to embody the public's conception of this figure. Base this embodiment on historical research into both fact and fiction concerning the character. Write a paragraph stating sources and pertinent information.

Daniel Boone	Queen Elizabeth I
Abe Lincoln	Mary Todd Lincoln
Davey Crockett	Dolly Madison
George Washington	Betsy Ross
Sir Walter Raleigh	Pocahontas
Benjamin Franklin	Priscilla Mullins
John Alden	Martha Washington
Benedict Arnold	Molly Brown
John Wilkes Booth	Lotta Crabtree

Songs might be obtained from:

Appelbaum, Stanley, ed. *Show Songs from 'The Black Crook' to 'The Red Mill'*. Original sheet music for 60 songs from 50 shows/1866-1906. New York: Dover Publications, Inc., 1974.

Birnie, W.A.H., Ed. *Reader's Digest Family Songbook*. Pleasantville, New York: The Reader's Digest Association, Inc., 1969.

Boui, Margaret Bradford, Ed. *The Fireside Book of Favorite American Songs*. New York: Simon and Schuster, 1952. (Contains music from before 1776.)

Silber, Irwin, Ed. *Songs of the Civil War*. New York: Columbia University Press, 1960.

Examples of such songs include:

Paul Bunyan "Way Down Upon the Water"
Molly Pitcher "Yankee Doodle"
John Brown "On Jordan's Stormy Banks"

Assignment 26
Grading Sheet

Evaluation of Musical Theatre Acting Project _____

Student _____ Date _____

Historical figure _____

Title of Song _____

Evaluation Scale: 4 Excellent
                      3 Very Good
                      2 Good
                      1 Fair

Comments	**Specific Ratings**	**Score**
	Choice of historical figure	
	Choice of song	
	Historical research	
	Physicalization of character:	
	a. appropriateness of posture	
	b. appropriateness of gesture	
	c. appropriateness of movement	
	Vocal technique	
	Grade Total	

Further Remarks:

_____

_____

_____

_____

Assignment 27

Select a costume piece appropriate for the historical figure you used in assignment 25. Describe accurately how you perceive the historical figure would be attired and coiffed while presenting this song. Discuss how the costume piece affects the presentation of the song and character. Discuss whether the addition of a prop would aid in the presentation of the music. For example, Mary Todd Lincoln would be dressed in a hoop skirt from the Civil War period. She might wear a shawl or carry a fan, which could be used in the presentation of a song. Her hair, in photos from the period, is most often pulled back tightly from the face with a bun at the nape of the neck. She might sing "When the Dew is on the Blossom," using the fan to help suggest the heat of a Southern summer day. Perform the song again using the costume piece and prop.

Grading Sheet

Evaluation of Musical Theatre Acting Project _____

Student _____ Date _____

Historical figure _____

Title of Song _____

Evaluation Scale: 4 Excellent
                      3 Very Good
                      2 Good
                      1 Fair

Comments   **Specific Ratings**   **Score**
                          Physicalization of character:
                          a.   use of costume piece
                          b.   use of prop
                          c.   appropriateness of movement
_____
                          Grade   Total
Further Remarks:

_____

_____

_____

_____

Assignment 28

Choose one five-minute scene which includes song. Select either a classic piece (e.g. Shakespeare's *As You Like It*, Goldsmith's *She Stoops to Conquer*) or a contemporary piece (*Butterflies are Free, Bus Stop*, or *Tonight at 8:30*). Discuss the affect of the music on the scene. Does it follow logically from the character? Does it enhance the situation or emotional content? Does it add humor? Does it detract from the scene? Can the scene be performed without it? Does the song require accompaniment? If so, what? By whom? Perform the scene.

Worksheet and Grade Sheet

Student _____ Date _____

Play _____

Author _____

Scene _____

Affect of Music on Scene _____

_____

_____

Evaluation Scale: 4 Excellent
                     3 Very Good
                     2 Good
                     1 Fair

Comments	Specific Ratings	Score
	Choice of Scene	
	Historical Research	
	Integration of Song	
	Performance of Song	
	Grade Total	

Further Remarks:

_____

_____

_____

_____

Assignment 28
Sample Scenes

Shakespeare's *As You Like It*:

Act II, iii
Jacques, Amies, and group

Act III, ii
Rosalind, Touchstone, Corin

Goldsmith's *She Stoops to Conquer*:

Act I, ii
Tony Lumpkin and the bar patrons

Sample discussion for *She Stoops to Conquer*:

Tony Lumpkin, a happy go lucky practical joker, is boisterous and extraverted enough to sing in public. The song establishes the rowdy quality of the tavern, and is humorous in content. The song can be cut or given to other characters: bar maids, patrons, tavern keeper, etc. The song does not require accompaniment but can have simple instrumental enhancement through the addition of guitar, lute, or tambourine. Accompaniment could be done by Tony or any other character in the tavern.

While the song could be cut, it does add to our perception of Tony's boisterous, less-than-cultured character. We see him in raucous interchange with lower class characters. The song shows us clearly the rowdy side of his sense of humor and the scene as a whole. During the eighteenth century "singing in the tavern" was a very popular pastime. The use of the song also serves to add energy to the scene. Simple choreography during the presentation of the song would add to the life of the scene as well.

Instructor comments or suggestions:

_____

_____

_____

_____

_____

_____

Chapter Eleven

PUTTING IT ALL TOGETHER
THE AUDITION

It doesn't matter what you know about the musical theatre genres if you can't get a role in one of them. Just as you succeed in performance if you analyze the musical play, you will succeed in auditions if you analyze the musical situation. First of all, unless the audition is for an original musical, research the history of the musical for which you're auditioning. If possible, find a copy and read it carefully. Classify it as to type. Obtain the score and analyze its layout. Examine carefully the songs of the character for whom you are auditioning. Analyze the layout of those songs. Listen to a recording of the production. If you're required to select your own audition material be sure to select songs which relate well to the production for which you are auditioning. If the audition scenes and songs are announced, familiarize yourself with that material. In either case, be prepared to sing the most difficult material from the production. Before you are cast, you will certainly be asked to display your ability to handle it.

Tape your audition music to no more than three pieces of cardboard for manageability. Each sheet of music should occupy one piece of cardboard. File folders work especially well if you have only two pages of music. Be sure music is clean and unstained. Note the key in color at the top of the music. Avoid music in difficult keys and rhythms unless you are allowed to supply your own accompanist. Note all cuts, additions, extended vamps, and rideouts legibly and in colors on your music. There is no need to sing an entire song, particularly if there is a great deal of repetition in the melodies of the verse and refrain. If your arrangement is too complicated to record on printed music, have it written out by a good copyist. Bring your own pianist, if possible. If not, be gracious to the accompanist provided. Don't

Figure 51.   An audition for ONCE UPON A MATTRESS *at the Phoenix Theatre. The gentleman with the scarf is George Abbott, reigning Broadway Musical Director for twenty-seven years. Seated behind him is his young producer Harold Prince.*

argue with him. Though you need him, he is employed by the director or producer. If he doesn't like your music, find out why. Be prepared to offer more than one vocal selection.

The serious musical theatre student should have a portfolio of audition songs. The portfolio should contain: two ballads which demonstrate vocal range so that those casting will immediately know how much vocal range is available to them; two rhythm songs which are uptempo but different in style; a show tune that is very theatre oriented and displays you as comfortable with energetic projection; a contemporary song (rock, country western, etc.) that demonstrates your special musical language; a patter song that displays your ability to handle lyrics; a "heavy" song that shows your ability to be dramatic; one or two comedy songs demonstrating your ability to amuse. This collection is ideal. You may not feel comfortable with all of the song types. You would never be required to do all of these types at any one audition. The portfolio does, however, contain a song for every audition situation, and you will feel comfortable knowing that you have some song prepared for any audition occasion which might arise.

If you can visit the audition space prior to the audition, do so. Observe the acoustics, levels, light, room color, room size (width, height, and depth), proximity of audience, and any possible distractions (windows, mirrors, doors, etc.). Practice your audition with a friend observing, if possible, to give feedback on how well you can be heard, etc. Do as many auditions as possible. You rehearse musical productions. Why not rehearse auditions?

Auditioning Do's
1. Warm up before you sing in as private a location as possible.
2. Keep your eyes up throughout your audition.
3. Sing an up tempo song first.
4. Sing what they want to hear. (Music related to the production.)
5. Dress so you can move and in order to enhance your particular physical attributes. Be particularly aware of choosing colors that make you look your best.

Auditioning Don'ts
1. Don't indulge in idle chit chat.
2. Don't do an overly recognizable song.
3. Don't do a signature song.
4. Don't do a song that has nothing to say.
5. Don't do a song that has no interest out of context.

6. Don't do a song requiring performance above and beyond the audition.

7. Don't do a song written by you or a friend.

8. Don't alter your dress or audition material if called back for later auditions.

In choosing monologues for auditioning, have a portfolio in the same way you have for the songs you prepare. The monologues should be no longer than 90 seconds. You should have a serious monologue. In choosing your serious selections avoid heavily realistic pieces as these do not occur in the musical theatre repertoire. Keep all your monologues to selections from musical theatre librettos. Do not write your own pieces. You should have a comic piece that emphasizes comic timing and the ability to handle language. You need another comic piece that shows the ability to tell a joke well. Another monologue from a Broadway opera or operetta should also be included. A final monologue would be one which shows you can change your physicality. As with songs, you would never be required to perform all of these monologues for any one situation but you would be prepared for any eventuality. Just as with songs, avoid the over-used material or material that is associated with a particular musical theatre performance. The Appendix which identifies audition songs is also a good reference for librettos which are less generally known. The primary things you want to be able to express in an audition are your ability to handle various kinds of material and your ability to make specific, clear choices.

Having completed the assignments in this text, you should be thoroughly prepared to approach the audition process. You should likewise be keenly aware of your strengths and weaknesses as a musical theatre actor. This text has shown how to continue to develop your musical acting skills and to overcome your weaknesses. So now on to your final assignment. Good luck with it and with your future!

Figure 52. SUNDAY IN THE PARK WITH GEORGE. *Courtesy of SHOWTIME.*

Final Exam

Prepare a 10 minute musical audition which shows your range as both an actor and a singer. Include three contrasting monologues and portions of at least three contrasting songs. (You may choose one or more pieces from a previous assignment that shows you at your best.)

Some appropriate choices might include:

Female Monologues

Dolly's farewell to Ephraim, *Hello, Dolly!*
Nelly's plea to Captain Brackett, *South Pacific*
Ado Annie's self description to Laurie, *Oklahoma!*

Female Songs

"I Love a Cop," *Fiorello* (comic)
"Marriage Type Love," *Me and Juliet* (rhythm)
"The Simple Joys of Maidenhood," *Camelot* (ballad)

Male Monologues

Cornelius' "Wonderful Day" speech, *Hello, Dolly!*
Alfred Doolittle's anti-marriage speech, *My Fair Lady*
Arthur's speech at the end of Act One, *Camelot*

Male Songs

"Floozies," *The Grass Harp* (comic)
"I'm No Girl's Toy," *Raggedy Ann* (rhythm)
"The Big Black Giant," *Me and Juliet* (ballad)

Final Exam
Grading Sheet

Evaluation of Musical Acting Project _____

Student _____ Date _____

Evaluation Scale: 4 Excellent
                      3 Very good
                      2 Good
                      1 Fair

Comments   **Specific Ratings**   **Score**

                      Choices of song

                      Choices of monologues

                      Arrangement of material

                      Physical differentiation between characters

                      Vocal differentiation between characters

                      Appropriate projection of characters

                      Appropriateness of movement and gesture

                      Understanding of selections

                      Appropriate use of energy

                      Vocal technique

                      Overall impression of audition

_____

                              Grade   Total

Further Remarks:

_____

_____

_____

Glossary

Air	is the musical space without lyric that appears between musical phrases of the song, between the verse and the chorus, after the vamp, and before the rideout.
Altitude	refers to the highness or lowness of a gesture.
Attainment	is the achieving of the character's super-objective.
An **Autistic Gesture**	is a movement which indicates the actor himself.
Automatism	is a comic device in which humor stems from lost human flexibility or behavior so often repeated that it becomes mechanical.
A **Ballad**	is a song with a recurrent theme, musically slower and longer than other show songs. It may be narrative, romantic, a soliloquy, or a character song.
Broadway Opera	emphasizes difficult music derived from popular sources. It is spectacular in content and treatment with little or no dialogue.
A **Charm Song**	features light, delicate music, and the music and lyrics are equally important. Charm songs are optimistic, shorter than other show songs, and often achieve much popularity outside the show.
The **Chorus**	introduces and develops the main melodic theme of the song. It is the most repeated section of the song.
Climax	is the moment of highest emotional intensity in the libretto.
Communicative Lyrics	are designed to excite the audience and involve it in the energy of the moment.
Concentration	is the ability to ignore all distractions and focus attention on the immediate requirements of the task at hand.
Crisis	is a complication, a moment of discovery for a character where a choice of action must be made.
A **Cross**	is a movement by an actor from one point on a stage to a new position on a stage.
Derision	is a comic device in which humor stems from poking fun at physical needs.
Diaphragm	is the dome-shaped muscle used for the support of vocal sound. It lies under the rib cage and separates the thoracic cavity from the abdominal cavity. The use of the diaphragm is crucial in the control of breath for sound.
Didactic Lyrics	instruct or give personal information about the character.
Dotted note	is a note having a dot at its right side, which adds to the note one half of its value.
An **Eleven 0'Clock Number**	is a showstopper scheduled late in the show to re-awaken the audience's enthusiasm. It is usually a star turn.

An **Emphatic Gesture**	is a movement which supports the text and serves as an exclamation point.
Flats	are used to indicate the key of a song along with sharps. A Flat notation next to a musical note on a staff lowers the tone one half step.
Flow	refers to the movement of a gesture into, away from, or across the body.
Goal	is the one thing the actor defines as most important to the character — what the character wants above all else. Also called "super-objective."
High Musical Comedy	is a type of musical comedy in which the dominant humorous element resides in the language of the text and the lyrics.
Humors	is a comic device in which humor stems from some imbalance or excess in character.
An **Illustrative Gesture**	pantomimes emotion, facts, or a demonstration.
Imagination	is the mental ability to project oneself into a different personality and a different locality.
An **Imitative Gesture**	copies or mimes the movement of another.
Incongruity	is a comic device in which humor stems from the juxtaposition of people, objects or situations which are obviously different, or placing characters in totally different surroundings, or placing the real in conflict with the ideal.
An **Indicative Gesture**	is a movement which points out a direction. Sometimes "Indicative" is used to refer only to movement pointing away from a performer.
Integration	associates something in the environment to the actor. It refers to the use of props, set pieces and costumes by an actor, as well as the tactile communication between actors.
Libretto	is the script of a musical. It is also called "the book."
Long Joke Comedy Song	has a careful narrative which builds to a surprise punch line. These are usually long songs, difficult to do.
Measure	is a group of beats set off by bar lines. The number of beats included in a measure is determined by the appropriate time signature.
Musical Comedy	is characterized by a loosely constructed plot, interspersed with extended bits of comedy business and vehicle numbers for specific, and often, non-related performing styles. There is little integration between music and libretto.
Musical Drama	is characterized by a score and plot which support each other. There is little or no extraneous material, and there are complex character development and integrated subplots.

Musical Farce	is a type of musical comedy in which humor arises from broad physical action and stereotypical characters. Plot action is generally very quick.
A **Musical Scene**	is a sequence which combines music, pantomime, dialogue, dance, or stylized movement.
Narrative Lyrics	tell a story.
A **Note**	is a musical symbol which indicates a specific tone when placed on a musical staff. Notes have different values which depend on the time signature. In a song where there are four beats per measure, the following note values would apply:

Quarter note	=	one beat
Half note	=	two beats
Whole note	=	four beats
Eighth note	=	one half beat

Objective	is the goal of the character at any given moment.
Observation	is the ability to perceive those specific elements which differentiate the actions of one person from another by studying people in the actions of their daily lives and at their emotional extremes.
Octave	is an interval embracing eight diatonic tones.
Operetta	is a romantic and lyrical form, having more music than dialogue, and featuring melodramatic stereotypes. Music is of primary importance with complex scores making frequent use of trios, quartets, sextets, and intricate choral numbers. Settings are often foreign.
A **Patter Comedy Song**	is a comic duet or solo in which the singers alternate verses or it is a quickly paced soliloquy in which the lyric is more important than the music.
Pitch	refers to the high-low quality of a musical tone.
The **Play with Music**	has few musical numbers and the plot is not dependent on the music. The musical numbers are often used to illustrate or comment on the action.
Range	is the term used to identify a voice type. It refers to the width of tones which a singer is capable of singing. Women's ranges include soprano, mezzo, and alto. Men's ranges include tenor, baritone, and bass.
Recall	is the process by which the actor draws on personal experiences identical to or similar to the character being portrayed.
A **Rest**	is a musical symbol indicating that for a specified time, the music and/or lyric cease. Rests, like notes, may have different values, depending on the symbol.
A **Revue**	is a combination of musical numbers, sketches, and routines based on a theme. Characters may or may not be continuing. The tone is sometimes satiric, sometimes retrospective.
A **Rhythm Song**	is primarily carried along or propelled by a regular dominant musical beat.

Rideout	is a reverse vamp. It ends each chorus and finally, the song, and can range from one to many bars.
Sharps	are used to indicate the key of a song along with flats. A sharp notation next to a musical note on a staff raises the tone one half step.
A **Short Joke Comedy Song**	features brief choruses, offering a repeated phrase at the end, thus allowing the audience time to laugh. The tone of the music is lighthearted and humorous.
A **song**	is the musical setting of a lyric.
The **Song Layout**	is the combination of vamp, verse, chorus, air, and rideout sections of a song.
Strength	refers to the force or weakness of a gesture.
Subjective Lyrics	involve the audience with the character's emotions or personal difficulties.
Subtext	is the meaning beneath the lyrics and the lines. It is the thoughts of the character at any given moment as interpreted by the actor.
Super-objective	is the goal of the character for the entire show. Individual objectives must be related to the character's super-objective. Also called the "goal."
Symphonic drama	is primarily patriotic or historic in plot and combines the elements of song, dance, drama, and spectacle. Music reflects the time and location of the production.
Tempo	refers to the speed of a movement, whether it is fast or slow.
Time signature	is a musical notation given at the beginning or within a musical composition to indicate its meter. One song may have more than one time signature.
Traditional Musical Comedy	describes a musical comedy libretto in which the humor lies in stereotypical, easily recognizable character types and illogical plot development which always resolves itself happily and generally with the boy getting the girl. Generally refers to librettos written before 1943. Also known as Classical Musical Comedy.
Triplet	is a group of three notes to be performed in place of one or two of the same value.
The **Vamp**	sets the key in which a song will be sung, the tempo for the listeners, and creates the environment of the song. Length depends partially on the time the singer needs to prepare for the song. The vamp may occur under dialogue which precedes the song.
The **Verse**	introduces and develops the subject of the song. It is melodically second to the chorus.

Audition Material

The songs included in this appendix are arranged according to appropriateness for certain ages and for either male or female voices. An attempt has been made to suggest material that is not overdone. Within the musicals suggested here, an actor might also find other songs in addition to the ones listed.

Young Juvenile (6-13):

"Be Kind to Your Parents" Harold Rome. *Fanny*. Bouncy, uptempo number. Some humor involved.

"The Older Generation" Rodgers and Hammerstein. *Flower Drum Song*. Bouncy, uptempo. Young people looking askance at older folks. Nice phrasing possibilities. Not difficult to sing.

"You're Never Fully Dressed Without A Smile" Charles Strouse. *Annie*. A lesser known piece from a well-known show. Originally sung by a chorus of orphans, it works well as a solo.

Juvenile (14-20):

"All I Need Is One Good Break" John Kander and Fred Ebb. *Flora, the Red Menace*. Driving, upbeat number.

"Dear Love" John Kander and Fred Ebb. *Flora, the Menace*. Bouncy waltz.

"Floozies" Kenward Elmslie and Claire Richardson. *The Grass Harp*. Uptempo number. Speaks of a young man's desire in a comic way.

"Imagine" Richard Rodgers, Lorenz Hart. *Babes in Arms*. Can be sung by male or female; easy, bouncy tune tells of looking for better times.

"Later" Stephen Sondheim. *A Little Night Music*. Though part of a trio, can easily be extracted and used as a solo. Primarily a male piece. Some difficult rhythms but an impressive piece.

"Mira" Bob Merrill. *Carnival*. Simple, honest ballad for strong, high soprano.

"Nice Little Jazz Bird" George and Ira Gershwin. *Lady, Be Good!* Nice, easy jazz syncopation for tenor voice.

"She's Too Far Above Me" Daird Heneker. *Half A Sixpence*. Ballad. Can be done with a cockney dialect but is also affective with Standard American pronunciation.

"Sing Happy" John Kander and Fred Ebb. *Flora, the Red Menace*. Belt (All of the numbers from *Flora, the Red Menace* are driving, energetic songs sung by Liza Minelli originally.)

"Treat Me Rough" George and Ira Gershwin. *Girl Crazy*. Bouncy tenor piece about a boy who wants to grow up. Some comic possibilities in an up-tempo second chorus.

"Without Me" John Kander and Fred Ebb. *The Happy Time*. Uptempo, optimistic number. Suitable for male or female.

"You Are So Fair" Richard Rodgers and Lorenz Hart. *Babes in Arms*. Tongue-in-cheek, bouncy ballad for male or female.

Romantic Lead (Female):

"Colors of My Life" Cy Coleman and Michael Stewart. *Barnum*. Originally a duet, this charming ballad can easily be a solo number.

"Come To My Garden" Marsha Norman and Lucy Simon. *The Secret Garden*. A haunting ballad from a recent musical, it is not yet overdone.

"Do I Love You" Cole Porter. *DuBarry Was A Lady*. Lovely, straight forward, little-known ballad. Though originally sung by Ethel Merman, the song works well with a legitimate voice as well.

"Don't Ever Leave Me" Oscar Hammerstein and Jerome Kern. *Sweet Adeline*. Haunting ballad requiring strong soprano range. Borders on torch song.

"If I Gave You" Hugh Martin and Timothy Gray. *High Spirits*. Another lovely, easy ballad.

"I Know Now" Ronald Millar and Ron Grainer. *Robert and Elizabeth*. From a British Musical, this dramatic ballad requires extensive female range. Though a duet, it can easily be an impressive solo piece as well.

"Love Look Away" Rodgers and Hammerstein. *Flower Drum Song*. Lovely, easy ballad.

"The Music That Makes Me Dance" Jule Styne and Bob Merrill. *Funny Girl*. Soulful ballad. "Torch song" quality.

"My Heart Belongs To Daddy" Cole Porter. *Leave It To Me*. The song which propelled Mary Martin to stardom; opportunities for humor and a suggestion of naughtiness for the would-be vamp.

"No Other Love" Richard Rodgers and Oscar Hammerstein. *Me and Juliet*. Well-known song but little performed piece calling for a full soprano range. Originally a duet, suitable for either female soprano or male tenor.

"Play A Simple Melody" Irving Berlin. *Watch Your Step* . Interesting piece combines an easy ballad and an uptempo syncopated counter-melody.

"Smoke Gets In Your Eyes" Jerome Kern and Otto Harbach. *Roberta.* Rather than singing it at the original uptempo, could work well as a torch song by slowing rhythm.

"Someone to Watch Over Me" George and Ira Gershwin. *Oh, Kay!* A lovely ballad; be sure to include the introduction to the piece.

"Speak Low" Kurt Weill and Ogden Nash. *One Touch Of Venus* . Another duet that doubles as a solo piece. Lovely ballad originally performed by Mary Martin.

"What Is a Man?" Richard Rodgers and Lorenz Hart. *Pal Joey* . Sentiment of torch song in bouncy ballad.

Romantic Lead (Male):

"Deep in My Heart Dear" Sigmund Romberg and Dorothy Donnelly. *The Student Prince* . Strong ballad for legitimate tenor. Originally a duet, works well as a solo piece.

"Finishing The Hat" Stephen Sondheim. *Sunday In The Park With George.* Requires strong musical skills, piece has demanding rhythms but is impressive.

"Hey There" Richard Adler and Jerry Ross. *The Pajama Game* . Flowing ballad for a baritone.

"I Am In Love" Cole Porter. *Can Can* . Love catches the singer unaware. Requires lyric baritone.

"I Do Not Know A Day I Didn't Love You" Richard Rodgers and Martin Charnum. *Two By Two* . Easy, pleasant ballad.

"It's A Lovely Day Today" Irving Berlin. *Call Me Madam.* Bouncy ballad for easy tenor range. Originally a duet, works well as solo.

"Just In Time" Jule Styne, Betty Comden and Adolph Green. *Bells Are Ringing.* Bouncy, easy ballad suitable for male or female; take it more uptempo as it is in the original.

"My Romance" Rodgers and Hart. *Jumbo.* Warm, romantic ballad. Little used but worth doing.

"Proud Lady" Stephen Schwartz. *The Baker's Wife* . Strong ballad from a charming, little known show.

"She Wasn't You" Alan Jay Lerner and Burton Lane. *On A Clear Day You Can See Forever*. Ballad. Easy Style.

"Sweet Danger" Robert Wright and George Forrest. *Kean*. A British import, this strong dramatic ballad was first sung by Alfred Drake. Requires a powerful baritone.

"Take the Moment" Richard Rodgers and Stephen Sondheim. *Do I Hear A Waltz*. Lovely, easy ballad.

"There Isn't One Girl;" Jerome Kern and P. G. Wodehouse. *Sitting Pretty*. Driving ballad about a young man feeling sorry for himself.

"Wish You Were Here" Harold Rome. *Wish You Were Here*. In the original, ballad has a Latin rhythm. Tenor can show higher register by singing the ending.

"Young and Foolish" Albert Hagree and Arnold B. Horwith. *Plain and Fancy*. Originally a duet, suitable for either solo tenor or soprano legitimate voices.

Character Female (20-40):

"Belly Up To the Bar, Boys" Meredith Willson. *The Unsinkable Molly Brown*. Originally sung by Tammy Grimes on stage and Debbie Reynolds on film, it's a rousing belt number.

"Find Out What They Like" Fats Waller and Andy Razof. *Ain't Misbehavin'*. Though a duet, works well as a solo. Bright, bluesy, "red hot", bouncy comic number.

"Ice Cream" Jerry Bock and Sheldon Harnick. *She Loves Me*. Using the convention of writing a letter, the song has real comic possibilities but shows high soprano range at the end.

"Never" Betty Comden and Adolf Green, Cy Coleman. *On The Twentieth Century*. Originally sung by Madeline Kahn, this number calls for a high soprano range and a very dramatic style.

"Old Maid" Harvey Schmidt and Tom Jones. *110 in the Shade*. By the same men who did *The Fantastics*, this dramatic piece shows a character trying to reconcile herself to never marrying.

"One Hundred Easy Ways" (to lose a man) Leonard Bernstein, Betty Comden and Adolph Green. *Wonderful Town*. Comic song originally done by Rosalind Russell, nicely combines singing and joke telling. Requires excellent comic timing and rapid speech.

"What Is A Friend For" Truman Capote and Harold Arlen. *House of Flowers*. Jazzy, rhythm song with some syncopation, originally performed by Pearl Bailey.

"Where Has My Hubby Gone Blues" Irwin Caesar, Otto Harbock and Vincent Youmans. *No, No,*

Nanette. One of the less known numbers from a popular production, this piece has an interesting torch song quality.

"You Took Advantage of Me" Richard Rodgers and Lorenz Hart. *On Your Toes*. Another well known but little performed ballad. An interesting twist would be to perform it at half time (as is done in the second half of the original) and really "vamp it up."

"You'd Better Love Me" Hugh Martin and Timothy Gray. *High Spirits*. A bouncy ballad from the zany adaptation of Noel Coward's *Blithe Spirit.*

Character Male (20-40):

"The Little Red Hat" Harvey Schmidt and Tom Jones. *110 In The Shade*. Bouncy, uptempo number, originally a duet, can easily be a solo.

"Once In Love With Amy" Frank Loesser. *Where's Charly?* Easy ballad originally sung by Ray Bolger, allows for much charm on the part of the performer.

"A Secretary Is Not A Toy" Frank Loesser. *How To Succeed In Business Without Really Trying*. Upbeat, bouncy number. Though the piece includes the chorus, it can easily be done as a solo.

"Think How It's Gonna Be" Lee Adams and Charles Strouse. *Applause.* A poignant ballad intended to convince, this is especially suitable for the 30-40 year old character male.

"Where is the Life that Late I Led?" Cole Porter. *Kiss Me, Kate*. Dramatic piece for legitimate baritone with nice opportunities for comedy and charm.

"You Are Beautiful" Richard Rodgers and Oscar Hammerstein. *Flower Drum Song*. An easy, soulful ballad.

Character Female (40+):

"After You, Who?" Cole Porter. *Gay Divorcee.* Torch song for low alto voice. "Bluesy," jazz feel to the piece. Good for 50+.

"Each Tomorrow Morning" Jerry Herman. *Dear World*. Strong optimistic ballad. Nice monologue between verses. Good comic possibilities.

"He Had Refinement" Arthur Schwartz and Dorothy Fields. *A Tree Grows in Brooklyn.* Great comic piece; might use Brooklyn dialect.

"Love Is the Reason" Arthur Schwartz and Dorothy Fields. *Cabin in the Sky* . Originally sung by Ethel Waters, using a more uptempo rhythm gives this song a more optimistic feel than usual.

"Moon In My Window" Richard Rodgers and Stephen Sondheim. *Do I Hear A Waltz* . Originally a trio, can be done as a solo. There is a lovely, wistful section in the number.

"One of the Boys" John Kander and Fred Ebb. *Woman of the Year* . Suitable for low alto, originally sung by Lauren Bacall, a nice uptempo, humorous number.

"Thank God I'm Old" Cy Coleman and Michael Stewart. *Barnum* . Works well for 60+ female. Bouncy, uptempo number. Has a comic flavor.

"Wages of Sin" Rupert Holmes. *Mystery of Edwin Drood.* Down-on-her-luck character sings this number that calls for audience participation in the original. Room for lots of fun. Requires low voice.

"When You're Good To Mama" John Kander and Fred Ebb. *Chicago* . Flashy, trashy belt.

"Wherever He Ain't" Jerry Herman. *Mack and Mabel* . Though this show never achieved the success of *Hello, Dolly* ! and other of Herman's work, it has many wonderful pieces including this driving belt number.

"Witch's Lament" Stephen Sondheim. *Into the Woods* . Mournful ballad, originally sung by Bernadette Peters.

Character Male (40+):

"How Can Love Survive" Richard Rodgers and Oscar Hammerstein. *The Sound of Music.* Certainly the show is a household word, but this number is rarely performed and, though a duet, can be easily done as a solo. It is an uptempo, breezy number.

"How Do You Do Middle Age?" Noel Coward. *The Girl Came to Supper.* A rueful though cheerful look at the middle years; peppy piece.

"I'm Glad I'm Not Young Anymore" Alan Jay Lerner and Frederick Lowe. *Gigi* . Another song for the older character male, this is a reflective, easy ballad.

"I'm Gonna Sit Right Down and Write Myself a Letter" Fred Ahlert and Joe Young. *Ain't Misbehavin'.* Can be sung by any voice, any age, at any tempo. An old standard but seldom performed.

"The Life of the Party" John Kander and Fred Ebb. *The Happy Time* . Grandfather sings this number in a rollicking bouncy uptempo style. Great fun for the older generation!

"Life's a Funny Proposition After All" George M. Cohan. *Little Johnny Jones*. Spoken musings on life and shows ability to stay with musical rhythm.

"Love is a Very Light Thing" Harold Rome. *Fanny*. Wistful ballad for a bass.

"More I Cannot Wish You" Frank Loesser. *Guys and Dolls*. Tender ballad. A number seldom done from a well-known musical.

"My Heart is so Full of You" Frank Loesser. *The Most Happy Fella.* Strong ballad for a legitimate baritone; the original is done with an Italian accent. Though a duet, can be done easily as a solo.

"The Olive Tree" Robert Wright and George Forrest (Based on themes of Alexander Borodin). *Kismet.* Reflective song of self discovery. Moments of driving rhythm for a strong baritone.

"September Song" Kurt Weill and Maxwell Anderson. *Knickerbocker Holiday*. Works well for 60+ male. Doesn't require a wide range. Nice, nostalgic ballad.

"Tulip Time in Sing Sing" Jerome Kern and P. G. Wodehouse. *Sitting Pretty*. Comic piece, fun lyrics, song of reminiscence and nostalgia.

"What Takes My Fancy" Cy Coleman and Carolyn Leigh. *Wildcat*. Though a duet in the original production, it works well as a comic uptempo solo piece.

Comic Songs (The following numbers are all comic in tone and offer much humor and fun for singer and audience alike.)

"Fiasco" Alan Jay Lerner and Andre Peorn. *Coco.* A humorous, snide, self-satisfied approach in a number reveling in the failure of another.

"Flash, Bang, Wallop" David Heneker. *Half a Sixpence.* Comic piece which allows for the possible use of cockney dialect. Bright, bouncy, uptempo suitable for any age male or female.

"Hand for the Hog" Roger Miller. *Big River.* Short number with a lot of punch. Knee slappin', foot tappin', rhythm piece suitable for juvenile through older character males.

"No Understand" Richard Rodgers and Stephen Sondheim. *Do I Hear a Waltz*. The premise of the piece is to give an English lesson to an Italian. Lots of room for comic interpretation.

"Something's Coming to Tea" Hugh Martin and Timothy Gray. *High Spirits*. Originally performed by the incomparable Bea Lillie, this patter song allows for use of standard British dialect suitable for Character Female. (30+)

for Character Female. (30+)

"What Do We Do? We Fly" Richard Rodgers and Stephen Sondheim. *Do I Hear a Waltz*. Though an ensemble piece, it translates easily to a solo number. Might employ the device of getting drunk during the course of the number, as happens in the show.

Songs for Dancers (The following numbers are suitable for dancers. They are not difficult to sing and require only minimal singing range.):

"Beautiful Candy" Bob Merrill. *Carnival* . Ballad, waltz tempo.

"I Might Fall Back On You" Jerome Kern and Oscar hammerstein. *Showboat*. A lighthearted warning for a lover to beware. Suitable for male.

"Money to Burn" David Heneker. *Half a Sixpence* . This song answers the question "What would you do if you won the lottery?" Male voice required.

"She's no longer a Gypsy" Lee Adams and Charles Strouse. *Applause* . A fun, lively number originally done for the chorus but works for either male or female solo.

"There is a Sucker Born Every Minute" Cy Coleman and Michael Stewart. *Barnum*. Very lively, bouncy number. Has the feeling of a strong sales pitch. Requires very high energy.

Figure 53. Show Boat, *Linda Michele and Terrence Monk as Magnolia and Ravenal in the Wedding Scene with Alan Young as Cap'N Andy. Courtesy Long Beach Civic Light Opera. Photo by Craig Schwartz.*

The following listings include only those musicals for which librettos may be purchased and omits those available only in rental, even though they appear in catalogue listings. We also omit those that may not be useful for class work. When there is more than one source we will show the publisher(s) or source for single editions and/or a major anthology. At the end of this appendix is a key to the abbrevations; a separate key for the Young Audience Musicals will follow Appendix III.

Allegro (Musical Drama): Little known and unusual story of a small town doctor's sojourn in the big city. Full of innovative and fresh material: "The Gentleman is a Dope," "So Far," "A Fellow Needs a Girl." **(SPR)**

Applause (High Musical Comedy): a witty look at the conflicts surrounding a Broadway musical, based on the movie classic *All About Eve*. Most of the characters are middle aged, but the script offers some taut confrontation scenes and monologues and the title song is rousing. Good for class studies. **(GMAT)**

Ballroom (Musical Drama): Middle aged characters in a story of a widow's romance at a meet and dance ballroom. Nice score, some touching scenes for young character actors. Good solo character studies. **(SF)**

Barnum (Musical Drama): Covers the career and marital discord of the great showman. Some very good possibilities for class work in the pantomime scenes and strong characterization development in individual numbers. A fine ballad, "The Colors of My Life," is much overlooked. **(FT)**

Ben Franklin in Paris (Musical Comedy): Some wonderful speeches and scenes for characters of varied ages and a nice robust score in this story of Franklin and his grandsons in the French court shortly after the American Revolution. **(SF)**

The Best Little Whorehouse in Texas (Musical Comedy/Drama): Rousing country music, strong scenes and speeches (one of those librettos that could play successfully without music, though the music is very good indeed) in this play about a small Texas town's madam and her clash with a TV evangelist. **(SF)**

Big River (Musical Drama): The adventures of Huckleberry Finn and Jim on the Mississippi. Not much for class scene work, some nice spiritual numbers for group work and reminiscent of the scores for Symphonic Drama. **(FT)**

Brigadoon (Musical Drama): Really enchanting story of love in parallel time, superb score, and both script and score have much opportunity for class work. Especially tricky is a long joke comedy song, "My Mother's Wedding Day." **(TGM)**

By Strouse (Revue): A fast and funny revue featuring music by the author of *Applause, Bye, Bye Birdie, Annie, Golden Boy,* and others. **(SF)**

Cabaret (Musical Drama): Sally Bowles is not the center of the stage play as she is the movie musical. Some nice opportunities for class work, particularly for character actors and accents. **(GMAT)**

Camelot (Musical Drama): Arthur and his courtiers bring the round table only fitfully to life. Some good duo scenes for class work but too well known to be used in audition; a lovely ballad, "Follow Me," has been ignored too long. **(FT) (GMAT)**

Carousel (Musical Drama): Turn of the century story of a New England carnival barker and his family offers strong script and score for class work. **(SPR)**

Celebration (Musical Comedy): The title song is the saving grace of the score and a wonderful chance for a class group effort, but this parable of age and youth is dreary. **(FT)**

Charlotte Sweet (Musical Comedy): Almost an operetta, this clever satire of an English music hall troupe is full of zany characters and musical delights for an acting class, good material for style exercises. **(SF)**

Chicago (Musical Comedy): Some fine songs: "All That Jazz," "Roxie," "Mr. Cellophane," and scenes and speeches in the story of a sensational murder trial in the windy city in the 1920's. **(SF)**

The Chocolate Soldier (Musical Comedy): A unique musical adapted from George Bernard Shaw's "Arms and the Man." The delightful story lends itself to some good individual characterizations. The songs are light and yet superb for exercises and auditions. Excellent scene work. **(PP)**

Cole (Revue): The life story and tunes of "The King of Broadway musicals"— Cole Porter. Marvelous material. **(SF)**

Company (Musical Drama): Story of a bachelor and his married friends offers a wide variety of interesting scenes and songs. Principally middle aged characters. **(FT) (TGM)**

Cowardly Custard (Revue): Contains the romantic music from Noel Coward's operettas as well as his musical comedy gems. Great material for exercises in tricky lyrics. **(SF)**

Curly McDimple (Musical Comedy): This satire on Shirley Temple movies allows students to work on mimicry and caricature. **(SF)**

Dames at Sea (Musical Comedy): A clever spoof of the old gold digger movies, in which every song sounds just a little bit like a hit from one of them. Great chance for classwork and observation practice. **(SF)**

A Day in Hollywood/A Night in the Ukraine (Revue/Musical Comedy): Act I has ushers in a 1930's style movie theatre lobby parodying the films and stars of the day; Act II imitates a Marx Brothers film. Act I is a wonderful showcase for specialty performers and Act II demonstrates imitative acting. There's a Jack Whiting musical medley and a fine blues number ("The Best in the World"). **(SF)**

The Desert Song (Operetta): Can young actors make much of the caricature roles in this story of desert marauders? It's fun to try, and the score ("One Alone," "Romance," "The Riff Song" and the title song) is a challenge. **(SF)**

Diamond Studs (Musical Comedy): Rip roaring country and western score in a comic tale of Jesse James. Great fun for young actors. **(SF)**

Doonesbury (Musical Comedy): Vignettes in the lives of the characters from the popular comic strip during their college days. Good chance to play characters who have been visually established in the minds of viewers. Weak score. **(FT)**

The Fantastics (Musical Comedy): Lovely score and some good chances for scene work in the story of the maturing of two young lovers. **(FT)**

Fashion (Musical Comedy): Clever script and score in the tale of a women's club which hires a professional director to stage the early American Classic. Lots of material for women and women in men's roles. **(SF)**

First Impressions (Musical Comedy): A musical version of *Pride and Prejudice* has a wonderful score and the music often reflects the 18th century setting. Good bet for style exercises and period costume work. **(SF)**

Follies (Musical Drama): A reunion of former follies performers gives them a chance to reassess their lives and loves. A memorable score for a wide variety of characters and accents. Scenes involving younger and older versions of the same characters offer strong class potential for scenes and characterizations. **(FT)**

Fiddler on the Roof (Musical Drama): Jewish residents of a Russian village are forced to emigrate. Accent work, drama, comedy, and a variety of challenging songs for class exercises, and individual development. **(TGM)**

Fiorello! (Musical Drama): The life story of New York City's controversial mayor offers some good acting opportunities and some superb comedy numbers. **(GMAT)**

Golden Boy (Musical Drama): Bitter story of a prize fighter has strong dramatic scenes and songs. Unusual material. **(SF)**

Good News (Musical Comedy): One of the musical comedy classics: The story of roaring twenties college kids features a memorable score: "The Best Things in Life Are Free," "The Varsity Drag," "Lucky in Love," the title song, and many more. **(SF)**

The Grand Tour (Musical Drama): A Polish Jew and an anti-semitic Polish colonel flee from the Nazis across war torn Europe. A wonderful and little known score, very strong scenes and good speeches. **(SF)**

The Grass Harp (Musical Comedy): Absolutely brilliant and little known score helps tell the story of a whimsical southern family embattled over a medicine recipe. Lovely and lyrical script. Good southern characterizations. **(SF)**

Grease (Musical Comedy): A spoof of the 50's Rock and Roll. Fun music appeals to all ages. Some of the subject matter and lyrics may be too strong for high school. Could be good for class exercises. **(SF) (GRM)**

Gypsy (Musical Drama): Plenty of material for young performers in this backstage story of the classic stage mother and her off-spring. **(TGM)**

Hair (Musical Comedy/Revue): Series of vignettes, now a period piece, set in the 1960's hippie revolution. **(GRM)**

Happy End (Musical Comedy): Satiric tale of Chicago gangsters and the Salvation Army features "Surabaya Johnny" and "The Bilbao Song." Strong class material. **(SF)**

How Now, Dow Jones (Musical Comedy): Weak story of a Wall Street romance, but some nice music and funny supporting characters. **(SF)**

I Love My Wife (Musical Comedy): Clever look at married yuppies integrates musicians with cast. Very witty lyrics. **(SF)**

Jerry's Girls (Revue): Jerry Herman's music from *Hello, Dolly!*, *Dear World*, *Mack and Mabel*, *Mame*, etc. in an all women package. **(SF)**

Jesus Christ Superstar (Broadway Opera): Story of the events of Holy Week offers challenge in vocal technique and in creating historical characters through music and lyric. Good scenes, monologues and class exercises. **(GRM)**

Johnny Johnson (Play With Music): Bitter anti-war story by the founder of Symphonic drama. Strong material. **(SF)**

King's Rhapsody (Operetta): Romantic story of a king and a commoner. Good operetta exercise. **(SF)**

The King of Escapes (Musical Drama): The fantastic formative years of the legendary Master of Escapes, Harry Houdini, told in a combination of magic and music. Good scene work; good monologues. **(PP)**

The King and I (Musical Drama): A British governess intrudes into the court of Siam in a musical rich with unique chances for musical theatre students. **(SPR)**

Kiss Me, Kate (Musical Comedy): American musical at its very best—bright, sparkling, energetic story of the love/hate relationship of two Broadway co-stars. Much material for class exercises and good audition numbers. **(TGM)**

Lady in the Dark (Musical Drama): Dated story of a lady editor's choice between career and romance, the script still offers some good acting exercises, and the difficult score includes some challenging individual and group numbers. **(GMAT)**

Leave It To Jane (Musical Comedy): Jane, the college widow, tries to get a star football player to play for the college under an assumed name. Some good songs and good scenes. **(PP)**

Leave it to Me (Musical Comedy): A good example of the 1930's musical comedy. Totally dependent on the personalities for whom it was created, this tale of international reporting offers only "My Heart Belongs to Daddy" to musical theatre aspirants. **(GMAT)**

Little Johnny Jones (Musical Drama): Cohan's first success about an American jockey in England who is accused of throwing a race, eventually clears his name. His horse is called Yankee Doodle. Great lead solo, good scenes and group work. **(PP)**

Little Mary Sunshine (Operetta): Actually this hilarious convoluted story of a beautiful young innkeeper in turn-of-the-century Colorado is a fine operetta spoof. Great fun, clever score. Good for class exercises. **(SF)**

A Little Night Music (Operetta): Some may challenge the classification, but the difficult score suggests the category. Good chance for class work in trios, quartets, and lieder, and short and long joke songs in this story of a 1900 country weekend, full of illicit romance and intrigue. **(GMAT)**

Little Shop of Horrors (Musical Comedy): Fun to play characters and a 1950s ambience make this a good bet for class work. Limited appeal in the score. **(SF)**

Lost in the Stars (Musical Drama): Brilliant and neglected score, strong acting scenes in this story of a black minister's fight for justice in 1950's British Africa. **(GMAT)**

Mack and Mabel (Musical Drama): Superb score, strong scenes and speeches in this musical about pre-talkies film director and star and their tragic romance. **(SF)**

Maggie Flynn (Musical Drama): Another overlooked score and script, both strong, tell the story of a young woman who runs an orphanage for black children in Civil War New York City. Lots of potential for inner city classes and workshops. **(SF)**

The Man With a Load of Mischief (Musical Comedy): Romance and intrigue at a 19th century inn. Stylish characterization, clever score. **(SF)**

The Me Nobody Knows (Revue): Ghetto children's experiences. Rock score. Very youthful, energetic material. **(SF)**

The Merry Widow (Operetta): High romance in Paris at the turn of the century. Lush, lovely score. Baron Popoff is anxious that the Prince marry the wealthy widow because the treasury is empty. Wonderful rehearsal material. **(PP)**

The Mikado (Operetta): Melodic, the Gilbert and Sullivan piece offers a comic view of Victorian Japan and arranged marriages. Excellent for class work. **(PP) (SF)**

Mame (Musical Comedy): One of the classics, but too well known in script and score to be worthwhile as audition material. Mostly middle aged characters. **(FT)**

Man of La Mancha (Musical Drama): Dramatic story of the imprisonment of Cervantes, from his novel *Don Quixote*. Superb speeches, scenes, and musical numbers. **(GMAT)**

Me and Juliet (Musical Comedy): Backstage antics of the "little people" involved in a Broadway musical. Unusual soliloquy ("The Big Black Giant") and other fine, little known songs ("Keep It Gay," "No Other Love") and scenes. **(SPR)**

The Mystery of Edwin Drood (Operetta): A good exercise in style playing in scenes and songs from this story of a Victorian murder. Offers the possibility for class work on audience interplay. (FT)

Naughty Marietta (Operetta): Marietta leaves Naples for New Orleans to avoid an unhappy marriage, in search of love and happiness. Fine score. **(PP)**

Nine (Musical Drama): Stage version of Fellinni's movie *8 1/2* has some interesting scenes and songs for students. Foreign locale and attitude offer some challenging research possibilities. **(SF)**

Of Thee I Sing (Musical Comedy): This is the first musical to win a Pulitzer Prize, and is a satire on a political campaign. Very dated and not a good bet for class work. "Love Is Sweeping the Country" and the title song offer some group possibilities. **(TGM)**

Oh BOY ! (Musical Comedy): A funny, yet believable, tale of modern marital misunderstandings with a bright score. **(PP)**

Oklahoma! (Musical Comedy): Good scenes and a wide variety of songs highlight the story of a cowboy and his sweetheart on the Oklahoma frontier. **(SPR)**

On the Twentieth Century (Musical Comedy): Extremely difficult score, good scenes in the story of a trainload of zanies, including a glamorous actress and an eccentric producer cross-countrying in the 1930's. **(SF)**

One Touch of Venus (High Musical Comedy): The goddess of love comes to life in 1940's Manhattan. Not very amusing today but offers a chance for class exercises, and a truly lovely ballad, "Speak Low." **(TGM)**

Over Here! (Musical Comedy): Musical version of the enduring fantasy about the boy who won't grow up and his Never-Never land. Good exercise in light touch and whimsy. **(SF)**

Pacific Overtures (Operetta): History of Japan offers some chances for stylistic playing in class projects, but not, in general, appealing in script or score. **(FT)**

The Phantom of the Opera (Operetta): A wonderful score highlights the favorite story of a monster's obsession with a young opera singer. Advanced voices only. Difficult and very challenging music. **(FT) (SF)**

Pippin (Musical Drama): Students like this script and score and it offers a chance at group effort in "Magic to Do" and solos in several introspective ballads. **(FT)**

The Pirates of Penzance (Operetta): Gilbert and Sullivan satire about apprenticeship and mixed-and-matched marriage. Great of its kind. **(PP) (SF)**

Plain and Fancy (Musical Comedy): Sophisticated New Yorkers among the Amish. Long neglected, fine score: "Young and Foolish" is a beautiful ballad; "Helluva Way to Run a Love Affair" is an excellent short joke song. **(SF)**

Porgy and Bess (Broadway Opera): A very familiar score, but beautiful, in this tale of a handicapped man's love for a cocaine addict, set against a southern ghetto in the 1920's. **(TGM)**

Promenade (Broadway Opera): Satirical look at the 1960's through the eyes of newly freed convicts. Some good group work possible. **(GRM) (SF)**

Pump Boys and Dinettes (Revue): Wonderful exercise in establishing mood and character solely through music. Country songs in a diner in Grand Ol' Opry country. **(SF)**

Purlie (Musical Comedy): Black preacher wants to build a church and establish freedom for his people. Strong score, excellent characterizations. **(SF)**

Raisin (Musical drama): Black family struggles to leave the ghetto. Strong scenes and speeches, adequate score. **(SF)**

The Revolution Machine (Musical Drama): A fun look at John Dickinson, the unsung hero of the American Revolutionary War period, best remembered for "not" signing the Declaration of Independence. Every word spoken by the character John Dickinson is an actual quote from his writings. Authentic and period-inspired music; very good source for scene, monologue and rehearsal work. **(PP)**

Robert and Elizabeth (Musical Drama): The love story of Robert Browning and Elizabeth Barrett offers strong scenes and a fine and unique score, with challenges for strong voices. **(SF)**

The Rocky Horror Show (Musical Comedy): A bit of everything (some not definable) in this camp of horror movies. Fun for students. **(SF)**

Runaways (Revue): Songs and speeches of troubled children and teens that offer some powerful material. **(SF)**

Seesaw (Musical Drama): Unlikely love story of a WASP lawyer and a Jewish dancer offers an overlooked but strong score and challenging scenes. **(SF)**

1776 (Musical Drama): Human drama in the Constitutional Congress with strong material for men of all ages. Also research opportunities abound here. **(TGM)**

Shenandoah (Musical Drama): Virginia farmer sees his family torn apart by the Civil War. Strong score, homey scenes, good exercises for Symphonic Drama playing. **(SF)**

Sherlock Holmes in the Deerstalker (Musical Drama): Music is in the style of turn-of-the-century British Music Halls. A delightful who-dunnit based on the book **Sherlock Holmes and the Arabian Princess**. Excellent scene work, strong monologues and interesting characterization studies. **(PP)**

Something's Afoot (Musical Comedy): Pokes fun at Agatha Christie mysteries. Original spoof and some nice comedy songs as weekend party guests are eliminated one by one on a mysterious island. **(SF)**

The Sound of Music (Musical Drama): The story of the Von Trapp family fleeing Nazi oppression is very well known, so is the music. Difficult for students to avoid copying other performances, but has good classroom opportunities. **(FT)**

South Pacific (Musical Drama): Generally overdone, but strong dramatic scenes and a brilliant score tell the story of American military men and women who were serving in the Pacific Islands during WWII. **(SPR)**

The Streets of New York (Musical Comedy): Version of the old melodrama about an unscrupulous banker preying on an innocent tenement family. Good style exercises. **(SF)**

Sugar Babies (Revue): Old time burlesque skits and musical numbers. Good style exercise. **(SF)**

Sunday in the Park with George (Broadway Opera): Intriguing story of artists, past and present. Difficult score and characters present good class challenges. The necessity of young performers aging in their roles presents a good learning experience. **(FT)**

Sweeney Todd (Broadway Opera): Difficult score in this story of a Victorian serial killer. Strong characters—good classroom work can be accomplished. Satire of melodramas. **(FT)**

They're Playing Our Song (Musical Comedy): Ups and downs of a songwriter and a lyricist in careers and romance. Nice, New Yorkish score, rather dated now but excellent for class work. **(SF)**

Tommy (Broadway Opera): No dialogue at all in this bizarre tale of a traumatized pinball wizard. Strong musical challenges. **(GRM)**

Tricks (Musical Comedy): Musical version of Moliere's *The Cheats of Scapin* offers a great chance for costume and style work as a clever servant sets out to solve his master's love problems. **(SF)**

Two Gentlemen of Verona (Broadway Opera): Dated rock version of the Shakespearean story of romantic rivalry. **(GRM)**

The Vagabond King (Operetta): "Only a Rose," "The Vagabond's Song"—fine, melodic score in this rousing story of a thief's romance with a court lady in 17th Century France. **(SF)**

Walking Happy (Musical Comedy): A Victorian musical about a bootmaker trying desperately to marry off his eligible daughters. Some cute scenes and a pleasant score, nice style possibilities for class work and solo characterization studies. **(SF)**

West Side Story (Musical Drama): Romance and rivalry in New York street gangs has aged well, and the show offers good class work with accents, movement, and complicated songs. **(TGM)**

White Horse Inn (Operetta): Pretty score, tuneful and not too difficult, romantic plot in 18th Century Virginia. Nice rehearsal for Symphonic Drama as well as operetta. **(SF)**

The Wiz (Musical Comedy): A multicultural *The Wizard of Oz*. Good material for class work. **(GRM)**

Wonderful Town (Musical Comedy): Fun filled story of aspiring actress and writer in 1930's Greenwich Village offers strong comedy numbers, a lovely ballad ("Quiet Girl"), and challenging movement opportunities. **(GMAT)**

Your Own Thing (Musical Comedy): Clever retelling of Shakespeare's *Twelfth Night* set in a disco. Nice comedy scenes, but is irretrievably late 1960's. **(GRM)**

Zorba (Musical Drama): Story of a young man's maturing in Greece with the aid of a philosophical mentor. Not much use in class work. **(FT) (SF)**

Key to Publisher/Sources:

(FT) Fireside Theatre   6550 E. 30th Street, P.O. Box 6325, Indianapolis, IN 46206-6325

(GRM) Great Rock Musicals   Check your library or used book stores. This is currently out of print. It is planned to be repinted; watch for it!

(SPR) *Six Plays by Rodgers and*   201 East 50th Street, New York, NY 10019
          Hammerstein
          Random House: The
          Modern Library

(TGM) *Ten Great Musicals of*   Check your library or used book stores. This is currently out of
          American   Theatre   print. It is planned to be reprinted; watch for it!
          (Stanley Richards)

(PP) Players Press   P. O. Box 1132, Studio City, CA 91614-0132 U.S.A.
                                     (818) 789-4980

                                     20 Park Drive, Romford, Essex RM1 4LH UNITED KINGDOM

(SF) Samuel French   25 W. 45thStreet, New York NY 10010-2751 U.S.A.
                                     (212) 206-8990

                                     52 Fitzroy Street, London, W1P 6JR UNITED KINGDOM

A is for Aesop. Kristin Lennox, Michael Bryant. A tuneful adventure based on the fable *The Lion and the Mouse.* **(PP)**

Aladdin N'His Magic Lamp. William-Alan Landes and Elbert McAlister. A magical fantasy based on the Arabian Nights classic. Marvelous character songs, good ballad, witty dialogue. **(PP)**

Albert the Machine. Robert Kenney and Bryan Williams. A frustrated computer with near-human emotions seeks to find his perfect employment. Light-hearted and entertaining songs. **(PP)**

Alice N'Wonderland. William-Alan Landes and Elbert McAlister.The fantastical adaptation of the children's classic of a girl traveling through the looking glass and into the magical land of wonder. Fun songs. **(PP)**

Annabelle Broom, The Unhappy Witch. Eleanor and Ray Harder. All about a non-conformist witch who would rather be chic; has lively dialogue and songs that blend charm and wit.**(MTI)**

Babes in Toyland. Victor Herbert, updated by Ken Holamon. Unforgettable tunes in this Herbert classic. Enjoyed by all ages. Requires strong voices. **(AP)**

Beanstalk! Joseph Robinette and James Shaw. Altered version of "Jack and the Beanstalk." Some nice scenes for class work and lively score. Some difficult rhythms. Needs trained voices. **(IE)**

Buttonbush. James P. McMahon and Nancy E. Ryan. A delightful fantasy about Timothy, the alligator, and his brothers being rescued by Clarissa, the frog, and her sisters. Lively score. **(PP)**

Charlotte's Web. Joseph Robinette and Charles Strouse. With a fun score from the composer of *Annie*, this is a real crowd pleaser. Some nice toe-tapping and foot stomping in "Welcome to the Zuckerman Barn." **(DP)**

The Cleverest Lawyer (or *Pierre Pathlin*). Margaret McKerrow, Michael Harrah, Roger Wertenberger. A musical adaptation of a classic French farce wherein a simple shepherd outsmarts a crafty lawyer. Simple songs. **(PP)**

The Fabulous Fable Factory. Joseph Robinette and Thomas Tierney. Delightful script based on Aesop's fables. Very tuneful, charming show. Suitable for all ages and groups. Very popular with audiences, a real gem. **(DP)**

A Frog King's Daughter Is Nothing To Sneeze At. Cheryl Thurston. A fantasy tale about a young prince whose attempts at winning the princess are foiled by his vicious allergies. Good ballad. **(PP)**

Huddles. Paul Collete and Robert Wright. A modern tale similar to *Alice In Wonderland* wherein Jenny's dolls and chores come to life the teach her the importance of assuming her responsibilies. Good music. **(PP)**

I Didn't Know That.   Johnny Saldance, Louis Maloney, Joyce Selber, Rachel Winfrew. Quick paced revue offering first facts and world records. Percussive accompaniment. Good for singers with little experience and lots of fun. **(AP)**

If the Shoe Fits. Victoria S. Peters, Pat Carson. A musical retelling of *The Old Lady Who Lived In A Shoe,* with marvelous tunes. **(PP)**

Jack N'The Beanstalk.   William-Alan Landes, Tom Cicero, David Cosio and Peace Wilson. A magnificent stage adaptation of the boy who grows a magic beanstalk. Lively score includes a lovely lullaby and fun ballads. **(PP)**

Just So.   Jan Silverman from Rudyard Kipling.   A play with music, one of the best adaptations of Kipling's work. Also includes chanting and rhythmic accompaniment. **(NP)**

Kiddledywinks!.   Joseph Robinette and Carl Jurman. A musical revue; works well for Junior High or High School groups. Requires only area staging. Lively score. **(DP)**

The Little Fir Tree.   Allison Woyiwada. A delightfully simple adaptation of the Hans Christian Anderson tale. Ideal for younger performers. **(PP)**

Melissa and the Magic Nutcracker. Joseph Robinette and Karl Jurman. Set at the turn of the century, shows how Christmas is celebrated in other countries. A spirited Musical. **(DP)**

Peter N'The Wolf.   William-Alan Landes and Gary D. Castillo. A unique adaptation of the classic Russian fable. Sparkling score includes a delightful song for the Wolf, our hero and a friendship song for all. **(PP)**

Peter Pan.   J. M. Barrie, Carolyn Leigh, Betty Comden & Adolph Green, Mark Charlap and Jule Styne. The wonderful musical originally starred Mary Martin. Good roles for children. A real crowd pleaser if you can handle the flying. **(SF)**

Rapunzel N'TheWitch.   William-Alan Landes and Paul Morse. A humorous adaptation of the classic story of a young girl locked in a tower by a Witch. Humorous songs, including several by the funny Witch, and two very good ballads. Good character development work. **(PP)**

The Revolution Machine.   Donna Marie Swajeski. A fact-based look at the American Revolutionary War as told through the voice of John Dickinson, the only non-signer of the Declaration of Independence. Period-influenced songs. Good monologues. **(PP)**

Rhyme Tyme.   William-Alan Landes and Jeff Rizzo. A musical look at Mother Gooseland, while she is away on vacation. Score consists of the traditional Mother Goose ryhme melodies arranged for easy vocalization. Excellent fun, lots of good scene work and character development studies. **(PP)**

Rumpelstiltskin. William-Alan Landes and Jeffrey Rizzo. Sensational stage adaptation. Rumpelstiltskin wants the Queen's first born only so he can have a friend. Score includes a dreamy love song, good ballads, and uptempo comic character songs. **(PP)**

Runaways. Elizabeth Swados. The focus is on troubled children of all ages. Good for high school groups. **(SF)**

The Secret Garden. Marsha Norman and Lucy Simon. Based on the novel by Francis Hodgson Burnett, this is a touching, powerful adaptation with two good roles for children. Appropriate for all ages. **(SF)**

Showdown at the Sugar Cane Saloon. Joseph Robinette and James Shaw. A spoof on old-fashioned melodramas. Use of stereotype characters; audience can boo and hiss. Light-hearted music but some tricky rhythms. **(DP)**

Spoon Rivery Anthology. Adapted by Charles Aidman. Master's poetry comes alive and songs from the period are interspersed including "The Water is Wide" and "Freedom." Works very well for high school groups. Music is not difficult and it is fun to sing. **(SF)**

Starmites. Barry Keating and Stuart Ross. A futuristic adventure with a pop rock score. High schoolers or junior high can have a lot of fun with this one. **(SF)**

Sunnyside Junior High. Allison and Rick Woyiwada. Modern influenced music highlights this score and book about young teenagers trying to fit into a new school. Very high energy, middle rock music style. Excellent scene, monologue, rehearsal and character development possibilities. **(PP)**

Tall Betsy and the Crackerbarrel Tales. Jacque Wheeler, Mariella Hartsfield and Ed Mobley. A lively ghost is the focus for the retelling of these Southern Folktales; has a bouncy score with piano and flute accompaniment. Works well for all ages. Good monologue, scene and class group work. **(PP)**

A Toby Show. Aurand Harris. Celebrates the "traveling tent show." American Folk style. Music of the period and "specialty" numbers for children of all ages. **(AP)**

Trial of Goldilocks. Joseph Robinette and Robert Chauls. An Opera for children. Tells the classic tale from several different points of view. **(DP)**

Try A Little Shakespeare. Frumi Cohen. A modern musical version of Shakespeare's *Comedy of Errors*. Score is highlighted by several high-energy, multiple voice songs. **(PP)**

Winnie the Pooh. A. A. Milne and Allen Friedman, adapted by Kristen Sergal. All the lovable characters with very singable music. Easy to produce. Works well for younger audiences. **(DP)**

The Wizard of Oz.   William-Alan Landes and David Cosio. Stage adaptation of the Frank L. Baum
fantasy of a young girl swept into the Land of Oz. Score has a beautiful ballad about a land
beyond the rainbow as well as high energy tunes including character songs for the Lion,
Tinman and Scarecrow. **(PP)**

Key to Publisher/Sources:

(AP)   Anchorage Press   P. O. Box 8067, New Orleans, LA 70182 (504) 283-8868

(DP)   Dramatic Pubnlishing Co.   P. O. Box 109, Woodstock, IL 60098 (815) 338-7710

(IE)   I. E. Clark Publishing   P. O. Box 246, St. John's Road, Schulenberg, TX 78956-0246
                                      (409) 743-4765

(NP)   New Plays, Inc.   P. O. Box 5074, Charlotteville, VA 22905

(MTI) Music Theatre International 545 Eighth Ave., New York, NY 10018 (212) 868-6668

(PP)   Players Press   P. O. Box 1132, Studio City, CA 91614-0132 U.S.A.
                                      (818) 789-4980

                                      20 Park Drive, Romford, Essex RM1 4LH UNITED KINGDOM

(SF)   Samuel French   25 W. 45thStreet, New York NY 10010-2751 U.S.A.
                                      (212) 206-8990

                                      52 Fitzroy Street, London, W1P 6JR UNITED KINGDOM

Albright, H.D., *Working Up a Part.* Boston: Houghton Mifflin Company, 1962.

Balk, Wesley. *The Complete Actor-Singer.* Minneapolis: University of Minnesota Press, 1977.

Benedette, Robert. *The Actor at Work.* Englewood Cliffs, NJ: Prentice-Hall 1976.

____ , *The Director at Work.* Englewood Cliffs, NJ

Blunt, Jerry. *Stage Dialects.* New York: Intext Publishers, 1967.

____ , *More Stage Dialects.* New York: Intext Publishers, 1967.

Bordman, Gerald. *American Musical Theatre: A Chronicle.* New York: Oxford University Press, 1978.

Bunch, Meribeth. *Dynamics of the Singing Voice.* 2nd, Revised Edition, Springer-Verlag, Wien, Austria.

Coger, Leslie Irene, and White, Melvin R. *Readers Theatre Handbook.* Glenview, IL.: Scott, Foresman and Company, 1982.

Collier, Gaylan Jayne. *Assignments in Acting.* New York : Harper and Row, 1970.

Corson, Richard. *Fashions in Hair.* London: Peter Owen, 1965.

Crawford, Jerry L. *Acting: In Person and In Style.* 4th edition. Dubuque, IA: Wm. C. Brown, 1991.

Crosscup, Richard. *Children and Dramatics.* New York. New York: Charles Scribner's and Sons, 1966.

Dean, Alexander and Carra, Lawrence. *Fundamentals of Play Directing.* 5th edition. New York: Holt, Rinehart and Winston, Inc., 1989.

Duffy, Natalie Willman. *Modern Dance: An Adult Beginner's Guide.* Englewood Cliffs, NJ: Prentice-Hall, 1982.

Doscher, Barbara. *The Functional Unity of the Singing Voice.*

Egri, Lajos. *The Art of Dramatic Writing.* New York: Simon and Schuster, 1965.

Engel, Lehman. *The American Musical Theatre.* New York: The Macmillan Press Publishing Company., 1975.

____ , *Getting the Show On: The Complete Guidebook for Producing a Musical in Your Theatre.* New York: Schirmer Books, 1983.

Fields, Alexander. *Foundations of the Singer's Art.* Jacksonville, Florida: National Association of Teachers of Singing, Inc., 1984.

Frankel, Aron. *Writing the Broadway Musical.* New York: Drama Book Specialists, 1977.

Grenbanier, Bernard. *Playwriting.* New York: Thomas Y. Cromwell Company, 1961.

Hagen, Uta. *Respect for Acting.* New York: Macmillan, 1973.

Hull, Carton.

Hunnisett, Jean. *Period Costume for Stage and Screen, Medieval to 1500.* Studio City, CA: Players Press, 1996

Hunnisett, Jean. *Period Costume for Stage and Screen, 1500-1800.* Studio City, CA: Players Press, 1991.

Hunnisett, Jean. *Period Costume for Stage and Screen, 1800-1909.* Studio City, CA: Players Press, 1991.

Jans, Martin, with Landes, William-Alan. *Stage Make-Up Techniques.* Studio City, CA: Players Press, 1992.

Jones, Frank Pierce. *Body Awareness in Action: A Study of the Alexander Technique.* New York: Schocken Books, 1976.

Kenney, James. *Becoming a Singing Performer.* Dubuque, IA: Wm. Brown Publishers, 1987.

King, Nancy. *Theatre Movement.* New York: Drama Book Specialists, 1971.

Kislan, Richard. *The Musical.* Englewood Cliffs, NJ: Prentice-Hall, Inc., 1976.

Kosarin, Oscar. *The Singing Actor.* Englewood Cliffs, NJ: Prentice-Hall, Inc., 1983.

Kuritz, Paul. *Playing.* Englewood Cliffs, NJ: Prentice-Hall, Inc: 1982.

Laughlin, Haller, and Wheeler, Randy. *Producing the Musical: A Guide for School, College and Community Theatres.* Westport: Greenwood Press, 1984.

Lessac, Arthur. *The Use and Training of the Human Voice.* New York: Drama Book Publishers, 1960.

McCaslin, Nellie. *Children and Drama.* Studio City, CA.: Players Press, 1997.

McGaw, Charles, and Clark, Larry D. *Acting is believing: A Basic Method.* 5th edition. New York: Holt, Rinhart and Winston, 1987.

McKinney, James C. *The Diagnosis and Correction of Vocal Faults.* Genevox, Nashville, TN, 1982.

Marshall, Madeleine. *The Singer's Manual of English Diction.* New York: Schirmer Books, 1953.

Mates, Julian. *The American Musical Stage before 1800.* Princeton, NJ, Rutgers Press, 1962.

Mielzner, Jo. *Designing for the Theatre.* New

York: Bramwell House, 1965.

Miller, Kenneth E. *Principles of Singing.* 2nd edition, Englewood Cliffs, NJ: Prentice-Hall, Inc., 1990.

Miller, Richard. *The Structure of Singing: System and Art in Vocal Technique.* New York: Schirmer Books, 1986.

Nielsen, Eric Brandt. *Dance Auditions: Preparation, Preservation, Career Planning.* Princeton: Princeton Book Company, 1984.

Oxenford, Lyn. *Playing Period Plays.* London: J. Garnet Miller, 1974.

Package Publicity Service, Inc. *Simon's Directory.* 1501 Broadway, Room 1314, New York, NY 10036. (212) 354-1480.

Parker, W. Owen, and Smith, Harvey K. *Scene Design and Stage Lighting.* New York: Holt, Rinehart and Winston, 1975.

Poulter, Christine. *Playing the Game.* Studio City, CA: Players Press, Inc., 1991.

Rawlins, Rich. *Look, Listen and Trust.* Studio City, CA: Players Press, Inc., 1992.

Richards, Stanley. *Great Musicals of the American Theatre,* Vol. 2. Radnor, PA: Chilton Book Company; 1976.

_____, *Great Rock Musicals.* New York: Stein and Day, Publishers, 1979.

_____, Ten Great Musicals of the American Theatre. Radnor, PA: Chilton Book Company, 1973.

Robertson, Warren. *Free to Act.* New York: G.P. Putnam's and Sons, 1977.

Rodgers, Richard, and Hammerstein, Oscar. *Six Plays by Rodgers and Hammerstein.* New York: Random House, 1963.

Theatre Crafts. Holmes, PA: Theatre Craft Associates, 1977.

Sable, Barbara Kinsey. The Vocal Sound. Englewood Cliffs, NJ: Prentice-Hall, 1982.

Shurtleff, Michael. *Audition.* Studio City CA: Walker & Company, 1978, distributed by Empire Publishing Services.

Spolin, Viola. *Improvisation for the Theatre.* Evanston, IL: Northwestern University Press, 1963.

_____. *Theatre Games for the Classroom.* Evanston, IL: Northwestern University Press, 1986.

Stanislavski, Constantin. *Building a Character.* New York: Theatre Arts Books, 1949.

Sunderland, Margot, with Pickering, Ken. *Choreographing the Stage Musical.* Illustrated by Phil Engleheart. Malvern, Worcestershire: J Garnet Miller, Ltd., 1990, distributed by Empire Publishing Service, Studio City, CA.

Figure 54. *Greg Louganis as the Prince and Juliet Lambert as Cinderella in Rodgers and Hammerstein's* Cinderella. *Courtesy of Long Beach Civic Light Opera.*

Accompaniment 10
Actor-Audience relationship 22, 101
Air 8, 9, 18, 43, 147
Alignment 24–25, 62
Altitude 25, 32, 91, 147
Attainment 99, 104, 105, 108, 147
Auditioning Do's 143
Auditioning Don'ts 143–144
Autistic Gesture 30
Automatism 72, 147
Ballad 7, 147
Bass Clef 10
Beat 10
Bolton, Guy 89
Breath 47
Breath Control 47, 114
Breathing Exercises 47
Brecht, Bertolt 132
Broadway Opera 5, 6, 119–122, 129, 130, 147
Character Female Songs (40+) 155–156
Character Male Songs (40+) 156–157
Character Female Songs (20-40) 154–155
Character Male Songs (20-40) 155
Character Motivation 102–103
Charm Song 7, 84, 85, 147
Chorus 8, 9, 12, 147
Classic Musical Comedy 71, 72, 95
Climax 99, 100, 104, 105, 106, 108, 147
Cohan, George M. 18, 50
Comedy Song 7, 143
Comic Songs 157–158
Communicative Lyrics 44, 147
Concentration 45, 60, 147
Concentration Exercises 46–47
Concept Musical 120
Conflict 99, 113
Contemporary Musical Comedy 73, 95
Crisis 23, 99, 100, 104, 105, 106, 107, 108, 147
A "Cross" 22, 147
Derision 72, 147
Diaphragm 10, 47, 147

Didactic Lyric 44, 147
Dotted Note 10, 147
Eleven o'Clock Number 7, 8, 147
Emotional Content 61, 101, 107, 115
Emphatic Gesture 30, 148
Energy 22, 28, 61, 63, 91, 97
Ensemble 2, 91
Flats 9, 148
Flow 32, 148
Forbush, Nellie 105
Gesture 21, 25, 30, 61, 115
Give My Regards to Broadway 49–53, 48
Goal 44, 99, 100, 101, 114, 148
Grading Sheets 19, 37, 42, 48, 54, 55, 67, 69, 90, 94, 96, 108, 109, 116, 117, 124, 127, 135, 137, 138, 139, 146
Green, Paul 130
Gypsy 43, 107
Hammerstein, Oscar II 134
High Musical Comedy 72, 73, 91, 95, 148
Humming 34
Humors 72, 148
Illustrative Gesture 30, 31, 148
Imagination 1, 44, 45, 133, 148
Imitative Gesture 30, 148
Improvisation 126, 134
Incongruity 72, 148
Indicative Gesture 30, 31, 148
Integration 71, 73, 99, 101, 120. 148
Introduction 8, 12, 32
Johnny Jones 50
Juvenile Songs 151
Kinesthetic Awareness 21, 61, 63
Leave it to Jane 76, 81
"Leave it to Jane" 76–80
Libretto 10, 44, 72, 74, 99, 101, 111, 130, 144, 148
Long Joke Song 7, 148
Measure 9, 148
Meter 150
Motivation 1, 71, 101, 102, 113
Movement 21–23, 95, 114, 125
Movement Analysis Chart I 33
Movement Analysis Chart II 36

Movement Terms 27
Musical Comedy 5, 70–74, 113, 114, 148
Musical Drama 5, 99–103, 104, 106, 108, 109, 113,
       114, 148
Musical Farce 72, 73, 74, 82, 95
Musical Phrase 47, 115
Musical Scene 8, 109, 113, 149
Narrative Lyric 44, 149
Neutral Energetic Posture 23, 24, 62
Note 9, 149
Objective 44, 106, 121, 149
Observation 44, 123, 133, 134 149
Octave 10, 149
Oh, Boy! 84, 85–86
"An Old-Fashioned Wife" 86–88
One Touch of Venus 93
Operetta 5, 6, 111–115, 119, 149
Pace Rehearsal 91
Patter Song 7, 143, 149
Personal Movement Analysis 36
Pirates of Penzance 6, 111
Play with Music 5, 6, 132, 133, 149
Physical Attitudes 25, 82, 114, 125
Pitch 10, 149
Posture 24–25, 28, 61, 62, 134
Range 10, 149
Recall 44, 45, 149
Relaxation 23, 126
Rest 9, 10, 149
Revue 5, 6, 129–130, 132, 149
Rideout 8, 9, 12, 43, 150
Rodgers, Richard 134
Rhythm Song 7, 143, 149
Romantic Lead, Female Songs 152–153
Romantic Lead, Male Songs 153–154
Sample Assignment Worksheets 81, 84, 93, 105,
       107
Score 114, 117, 120, 121, 130, 141
Sense Recall 45, 85
Shaking 30, 34, 63
Sharps 9, 150
She Stoops to Conquer 131, 139, 140
Short joke Song 7, 150

Show Layout 7, 8, 141
Show Type 5, 7, 8, 141
Sighing 35
Sondheim, Stephen 120, 134
Song Layout 8, 12, 141, 150
Songs for Dancers 158
South Pacific 105
Stanislavsky, Konstantin 2
Strength 32, 150
Stretching 29, 34
Student Worksheets 64, 65, 75, 83, 92, 123, 125,
       139
Subjective Lyrics 44, 150
Subtext 2, 43, 44, 102, 106, 107, 115, 121, 150
Super-Objective 44, 84, 99, 100, 104, 105, 106,
       107, 150
Swallowing 34
Symphonic Drama 5, 6, 130, 133, 150
Tactics 101
Tempo 32, 150
Tension 23, 34
Throughline of Action 100, 104, 105
Time Signature 9, 43, 150
Traditional Musical Comedy 72, 150
Treble Clef 10
Triplet 10, 150
Vamp 8, 12, 43, 150
Verse 8, 9, 12, 43, 150
Vocal Warm-up Exercises 34
Vocalize 10
Yawning 28, 34, 35
Young Juvenile Songs 151
Warm-up Exercises for the Body 23, 28–30
Webber, Andrew Lloyd 118, 120, 130
When Frederic Was a Little Lad 39–41
Wodehouse, P. G. 86, 89
The Yankee Doodle Boy 12, 13–18

Additional PLAYERS PRESS *Books:*

THEATER GAMES/IMPROVISATION

Playing the Game Christine Poulter   ISBN 0-88734-611-1

101 Theatre Games Mila Johansen   ISBN 0-88734-911-0

Look, Listen and Trust George Rawlins & Jillian Rich ISBN 0-88734-618-9

MONOLOGUES AND SCENES

Scenes for Acting & Directing Samuel Elkind
    vol 1 ISBN 0-88734-617-0   **vol 2** ISBN 0-88734-623-5

Absurd, Black and Comic Sketches Peter Joucla ISBN 0-88734-613-8

Performance One   William-Alan Landes   ISBN 0-88734-122-5

Monologues and Scenes from World Theatre Edited by William-Alan Landes
    vol 1 Ancient Greek & Roman   ISBN 0-88734-125-X
    vol 2 German, French, Spanish, Italian, Russian ISBN 0-88734-126-8
    vol 3 Belgian, Austrian, Scandinavian, Irish   ISBN 0-88734-127-6
    vol 4 English   ISBN 0-88734-128-4
    vol 5 American   ISBN 0-88734-129-2

Short Scenes from Shakespeare Samuel Selden & William-Alan Landes
                                                ISBN 0-88734-632-4

TECHNICAL THEATRE

Corrugated Cardboard Scenery Daryl M. Wedwick & Briant Hamor Lee ISBN 0-88734-628-6

Stage Make-Up Techniques Martin Jans and William-Alan Landes   ISBN 0-88734-621-9

How To Make Historic American Costumes Mary Evans & William-Alan Landes
                                                ISBN 0-88734-636-7

Western European Costumes Iris Brooke & William-ALan Landes   ISBN 0-88734-635-9

Stagecrafters' Handbook   I. E. Clark   ISBN 0-88734-649-9

PERFORMING

Principles of Stage Combat Claude D. Kezer   ISBN 0-88734-650-2

Wild West Country Dancing Mika Nurminen   ISBN 0-88734-652-9

American Musical Theatre   Steven Porter   ISBN 0-88734-684-7

The Drama and Theatre Arts Course Book
                    David Self   ISBN 0-88734-639-1

SHAKESPEARE

Shakespeare's Quotations Trevor R. Griffiths/Trevor A. Joscelyne   ISBN 0-88734-620-0

Shakespeare's Characters Kenneth McLeish   ISBN 0-88734-608-1

Shakespeare Two Thousand Fannie Gross/William-Alan Landes   ISBN 0-88734-626-X

Available at your local bookstore or contact:

PLAYERS PRESS P.O. Box 1132, Studio City, CA 91614-0132 U.S.A.
                 20 Park Drive, Romford, Essex, RM1 4LH, United Kingdom